DISCARD

D1360194

BLONDE

RATTLESNAKE

BLONDE
RATTLESNAKE

BURMAH ADAMS, TOM WHITE, AND THE 1933 CRIME SPREE THAT TERRORIZED LOS ANGELES

JULIA BRICKLIN

Guilford, Connecticut

An imprint of The Rowman & Littlefield Publishing Group, Inc.
4501 Forbes Blvd., Ste. 200
Lanham, MD 20706
www.rowman.com

Distributed by NATIONAL BOOK NETWORK

Copyright © 2019 Julia Bricklin

All rights reserved. No part of this book may be reproduced in any form or by any electronic or mechanical means, including information storage and retrieval systems, without written permission from the publisher, except by a reviewer who may quote passages in a review.

British Library Cataloguing-in-Publication Information available

Library of Congress Cataloging in Publication Data available

ISBN 978-1-4930-3789-6 (hardcover)
ISBN 978-1-4930-3790-2 (e-book)

♾™ The paper used in this publication meets the minimum requirements of American National Standard for Information Sciences—Permanence of Paper for Printed Library Materials, ANSI/NISO Z39.48-1992.

Printed in the United States of America

CONTENTS

AUTHOR'S NOTE

In 1938 RKO Radio Pictures released a film called *Condemned Women*. It starred Sally Eilers as Linda Wilson, a young woman sentenced to three years in a penitentiary for shoplifting. The character tries to kill herself on the way to prison, and a young psychiatrist played by Louis Hayward not only saves her life but also endeavors to change her embittered and hopeless outlook on it. Before long, doctor and inmate fall in love and plan to marry once Wilson is released. Every movie needs conflict, and in *Condemned Women* this conflict is developed when the warden convinces young Linda that marrying a felon would ruin the psychiatrist's fledgling career. And so Eilers's character joins a jailbreak attempt, hoping this will quash his love for her.

The picture was filmed at the California Institution for Women at Tehachapi. Director Lew Landers decided to use real inmates as background actors. "So savage was the fight," wrote one movie gossip reporter of the jailbreak scene, "it was whispered about that maybe a few of the extra girls might be paying off a grudge."[1] If one looks very closely at that scene where ninety-five women are screaming and bouncing off one another like atoms heated to boiling, one can see in the crowd of women a blonde, bobbed woman with nearly bulbous eyes and a pert, upturned nose. If one looks even more closely, one can see her smiling. This would-be actress is Burmah Adams White.

White's smirk in *Condemned Women* doesn't look all that odd. All the other inmates-turned-thespians-for-a-day had some sort of goofy, unnatural look that movie extras sometimes wear. But it was this smile that played such a big part in the reason Burmah was in Tehachapi in the first place.

The filmmakers did not credit any of its "inmate extras," famous or not. In fact, I only found the film because I was trying to find a documentary about Tehachapi for general research. Ironically, just a few years prior to the commencement of filming of *Condemned Women*, thousands of newspapers and dozens of radio stations covered Burmah's crimes, trial, and incarceration. Everybody in America knew the story of Los

Angeles's "girl bandit," even while more violent crimes captured the country's imagination as well that summer and fall of 1933. In the Midwest, Bonnie and Clyde were in the middle of a murderous two-year bank-robbing spree; in Chicago a Lindbergh baby–kidnapping suspect was arrested. During the so-called Kansas City Massacre in June of that year, three gunmen fatally ambushed a group of unarmed police officers and FBI agents escorting bank robber Frank Nash back to prison. In July 1933, George "Machine Gun Kelly" Barnes kidnapped Oklahoma oilman Charles Urschel.

But the wayward teen from a small town south of Los Angeles was a little different. She represented America's growing obsession with youth and lawlessness. "The recent conviction of Burmah White, 19-year-old girl bandit," wrote the *Los Angeles Times*, "emphasizes the startling fact that youngsters now comprise the most prolific crime group." During the first half of 1933, the year considered the peak of the Great Depression, one in five arrests for felonies was a person under age twenty-one. Three-fifths of all arrested for felonies were under the age of thirty. Burmah belonged to a special class: Only 7 percent of all arrested were female.[2] Responsibility for youth who commit crimes lay squarely with the parents, wrote the *Times* as well as many studies done at that time. "Too many fathers," the *Times* opined, "are too busy in the pursuit of money or in making a name to realize that their real wealth and worth are in the manhood of the youth for whom they are responsible. The records show that many of the boys and girls who go wrong come from broken homes."[3]

This was not the case with Burmah Arline Adams White. Her parents were resolutely, perhaps even happily, married. In spite of having the same financial hardships that afflicted the rest of the country during the financial crisis, the Adamses worked very hard to provide a good home in a safe neighborhood with well-funded public schools. Other than her attractive looks and above-average intelligence, Burmah Adams was not really different from most suburban teenagers.

When I first started researching and writing this book, I assumed I would come to some conclusion about Burmah White's motivations for participating in crime with her husband and the seemingly odd behavior she presented while robbing victims and during her trial. There were so many factors to choose from: young age, mental and/or physical abuse, drugs or alcohol or both, head trauma caused by a childhood accident, a desire to provide for her family, a desire for nice things, a combination of some of these or all of these. Or . . . none of these.

I still don't know.

INTRODUCTION

On Wednesday, August 16, 1933, Charles "Crombie" Allen took his companion, Cora Withington, to see the film *Tugboat Annie* at Loew's State Theater in Los Angeles. The show ended at about 9:30 at night. Knowing how much she wanted to learn how to drive, Allen let Withington take the wheel of his new Chevrolet coupe. As she gingerly slowed at a stoplight at Third Street and Lafayette Park Place, a car suddenly appeared next to theirs. A man jumped out of its passenger side, brandished a gun in the couple's faces, and said, "Shell out, sweetheart! And that goes for you too, Bo!" After Allen turned over his watch and the eighteen dollars he had in his pocket, his terrified companion started to hand over her purse. "The first thing I knew," Allen later said, "there was an explosion—and I felt a sting in my neck."[1]

Allen did not realize until a few moments later that the bullet that sliced his neck was the same one that tore through Withington's left eye and came out close to her right one. The shy, fifty-two-year-old schoolteacher was slumped forward onto the steering wheel, bleeding from her temple. A nanosecond before he realized his companion was gravely wounded, Allen noticed the strangest thing: The driver of the robber's car was a young woman with platinum blonde hair peeking out from a brown scarf, and . . . she was laughing as they screeched away.

Leslie Thomas Bartel, a bond salesman who lived one mile away on Third Street and South Kenmore, was horrified to learn later that his green, five-passenger Graham Eight sedan was used in the crime. While he was chatting outside with a neighbor earlier in the day, a man and woman had driven up and demanded cash and the keys to Bartel's car; they left behind a gray Chevrolet coupe that belonged to Nick Steponovich of Lawndale, whom they also had robbed at gunpoint. Bartel noticed that both the bandit and the woman driving the car wore horn-rimmed dark sunglasses, and additionally that the woman wore a brown turban-type scarf with platinum blonde hair wisping out at the bottom.

Bartel got his car back the next day; police found it abandoned several miles away. On August 22, in an effort to identify the man who so wantonly shot Allen and Withington, police asked Bartel, along with other robbery victims, to come in and look at no fewer than 127 criminal suspects they had rounded up from around the city—to no avail. That day and evening, a couple who resembled descriptions given to the police robbed seven other people. One of them, Jo Robinson, slowed for a traffic light at the major intersection of Pico Boulevard and Norton Avenue; as he did so, another car drove alongside and forced him to the curb. A man, leveling a pistol, stepped onto Robinson's running board and forced him to hand over ten dollars. And G. M. Gardener was held up by a man and woman who drove into the service station of his mechanic's garage on San Marino Street and Vermont; the criminals took all his earnings from the week—eighty dollars.

By this time it was public knowledge that the male robber had shot Allen and Withington even though the teacher was obviously handing over her belongings—when her purse snagged on a skirt thread, he shot the woman for being impertinent and slow. On August 26 this vicious couple went on another spree in which they relieved—at gunpoint—several people and grocery stores of cash. The most they got that day was sixty-five dollars, from Reuben Erdmann, a carpenter who lived on Occidental Boulevard.

Five days later, on August 31, the criminal pair pulled up to an apartment building at 227 South Western Avenue. As the woman waited in the idling car, the man stealthily followed Clarence C. Lewis into the front door of the structure, grabbed him around the chest from behind with one arm, and put a pistol to his temple with the other. "Empty your pockets," the robber tried to say. Before he could finish the sentence, Lewis wormed out of his embrace, turned around, and punched the man in the jaw. The bandit fired two wide shots as he stumbled and ran back to the car. His blonde chauffeur peeled away. About twenty minutes later, according to police reports, the maroon coupe pulled up in front of a Safeway grocery store at 3126 West Tenth Street. Leaving the woman in the car, the man entered the store and forced manager Jack Hanford into a rear room, bound and gagged him, and took the contents of the cash register, about forty dollars.[2]

These were but a few of the crimes committed by Thomas N. White, age twenty-eight, and Burmah Arline Adams, age nineteen. They committed at least a dozen more felonies between August 1 and September 1, 1933, and probably carried out more than twenty. But in many of the cases, the victims could not make a solid identification. In almost every instance, the victim or victims were distracted either by the woman's striking appearance or by her seeming indifference to the crime or both. For example, as his robbers drove away, Jo Robinson took a good long look at the blonde woman driving the car. He was certain that—based on descriptions in the newspapers and radio—she was the accomplice who laughed as her beau pulled the trigger on the schoolteacher and her publisher friend. She laughed at Robinson too.

It was, in part, this laughter—this real or perceived callous disregard for the heinous crime she had helped commit—that spurred the Los Angeles Police Department to launch the biggest manhunt the city had seen since two years before, when the LAPD was looking for four men who had robbed the Security First National Bank in Belvedere Gardens and killed a customer. The consortium of police, sheriffs, and lawmakers put together by District Attorney Buron Fitts used Adams and White as an example of why it needed to take extraordinary measures against criminals, including a blanket indictment and a fifty-thousand-dollar bond for any person arrested who was suspected of gang activity. "The grand jury and this office," said Fitts, "intend to make life in Los Angeles unbearable for known gangsters. We intend to make the gangster virtually a man without a country."[3]

This meant women as well. Burmah was taken into custody after her husband was killed in a shootout with police on September 6, 1933, ending a reign of terror that spanned a mere six weeks but pushed Los Angeles to the far edge of anxiety. Burmah was not Bonnie Parker. She was not part of a gang that targeted banks or capitalist institutions. She was not part of a crew that used violence to draw attention to social injustice. Rather, Burmah Adams White was a beautiful, intelligent, educated woman raised by a loving family. She had helped the family stay solvent in spite of the hardships of the Depression, and seemingly had no reason to engage in such violence. In other words, she was the most dangerous kind of criminal—perhaps even a sociopath.

Nettie J. Yaw, the sheriff's deputy who had charge of Burmah during her trial, assessed her as one of a certain type of female criminal: the "thrill-girl." "I do not believe prison means anything to her but another thrill," Yaw wrote for the *Los Angeles Times Sunday Magazine* in March 1934. This type, she continued, possessed a "sublime ego that absolutely obliterates any thoughts of the rights of others, the consequences of acts. Pleasures, pain, new drinks, new romances, new adventures make up their lives." If the "courage and sangfroid" of such women could just be turned in the right direction before it was too late, Yaw mused, they could become "avarices with world-class ambitions." Unfortunately, she added, some have "an added cold-blooded indifference to brutality and bloodshed that is appalling."[4]

Burmah Adams White committed her crimes when there were four inherent strikes against her. First, 1933 was the peak year of the Great Depression, and for many working-class families like her own, there was simply no money to hire an attorney of one's choosing or of a certain caliber. Burmah's parents, like the ones of so many other young people, were unable to work consistently. Every dime went to household expenses like food and rent.

Second, Los Angeles (and the country at large) was experiencing an epic crime wave, with homicide and bank robberies at an all-time high and a public that was desperate for law and order. For many people, according to one historian, crime had come to symbolize deeper structural problems of a society whose values seemed wildly askew.[5]

Third, police killed Burmah's husband, who had committed the actual violence, leaving his widow to absorb the wrath of a public that felt helpless. And yet, some citizens were frightened of the crime but also captivated by it. They followed the exploits of such outlaws as "Baby Face" Nelson, "Machine Gun Kelly" Barnes, and Clyde Barrow and Bonnie Parker, whose daring exploits provided a vicarious outlet for their own "antiauthoritarian impulses." "In this potentially unstable climate," argues Cairns, "some politicians sought to capture both audiences, touting tough-on-crime policies for the former [those worried about societal values] and imposing harsh sentences to remind the latter [those captivated by daring exploits] of the perils of flouting authority."[6]

Finally, Burmah went along with the crime when newspapers were desperate for sensation that would help them survive the Depression and when radio broadcasting companies were competing with one another for bigger pieces of a national audience. The teen's sad but superficially romantic story provided plenty of fodder for these media outlets. In fact, a coterie of newspaper reporters were invited to accompany the LAPD into the Whites' apartment building to bear witness to the capture of the pair. Stories of "female outlaws" were even more popular: Women who seemed to live by their own rules and life choices received significant attention during the Depression from members of the media, who were eager to play up the seductive and sexually titillating aspects of their exploits. Los Angeles newspapers, for example, still wrote about "tiger-woman" Clara Phillips in 1933, eleven years after her conviction, reminding readers of her sexual relationship with a smitten court-watcher who helped her escape after her murder conviction.[7]

Tom and Burmah's crime spree pushed Angelenos to their limit. On September 11, 1933, District Attorney Buron Fitts announced that the County Board of Supervisors had passed an emergency ordinance requiring all felons who had acquired a record during the prior ten years to register with the sheriff's department and provide fingerprints, physical descriptions, photographs, statements of their crimes, and current addresses. Moments earlier, Fitts had announced a resolution by the grand jurors commending LAPD Chief James E. Davis and the officers who "shot and killed Thomas White, the bandit who terrorized the city for twenty nights, and captured his blonde wife, Burmah White." The Los Angeles City Council followed suit the next day, also passing an ordinance that required all persons who had been convicted of a felony within the prior ten years to register with the LAPD.[8] These ordinances—precursors of Los Angeles's modern-day criminal database—were a direct result of Tom White's criminal acts.

The Whites were the catalyst not only for a new criminal tracking system but also for new sentencing guidelines. Judge Fletcher Bowron, who would become mayor of Los Angeles in 1939, said he had no choice but to make an example out of Burmah:

It is not a pleasant duty to send a young person, and particularly a young woman, to the penitentiary. As an individual I have nothing but heartfelt sympathy and pity for this young woman who is about to be branded a convict. But as a judge, my duty is plain. Burmah White, the penalty I am about to impose is not retribution. . . . But it is hoped that your case will serve as an object lesson to others.

And with this proclamation, on November 7, 1933, Judge Bowron sentenced Burmah to thirty years to life at San Quentin State Prison. The next day, the *Los Angeles Times* printed an addendum to Bowron's lecture from the day before, in which the judge lamented the fact that Burmah could be eligible for parole in as little as three years and three months. "In the first place," said Bowron, "the fixing of sentence and determination of the length of the prisoner must remain within the prison is so far removed from the scene and the time of conviction, and is fraught with so much uncertainty and secrecy, that punishment has largely lost its deterrent effect."[9]

Burmah's conviction and sentencing spurred ambitious judges and political leaders in Los Angeles to agitate for an overhaul of the parole system, which until this time had been "secret"—that is, the California State Board of Prison Terms and Paroles determined the length of a prisoner's incarceration with no input from a trial judge or a public hearing or even notification to those parties. "The people of this State," continued Bowron, "should demand a change in the present laws so as to provide proper punishment without secret or ill-considered parole."[10]

For Bowron, Burmah White personified the worst kind of villain: one who had every reason to avoid a life of crime and who had been insulated from the worst effects of the Great Depression by way of a good family. When pronouncing her sentence at the end of her sensational trial in November 1933, the jurist opined, "She had the advantage of a good home and was reared by honest and respected parents. She is intelligent and had a fair education. Thereafter, she deliberately chose a life of crime."[11]

Neither Burmah nor Tom had any children, so there are no descendants to give insight to their lives before, during, and after their crimes and deaths. Their exploits were so notorious that their siblings changed their names and moved to other states. But there was plenty of newspaper coverage, both straightforward and sensational. Newly digitized radio program transcripts provide a glimpse of the public's reaction to Burmah and Tom's lawlessness, and reconstructed genealogies place them in the human family rather than just figures on a newspaper page. Author interviews with descendants of politicians, prison trustees, victims, and more distant relatives of the couple reveal multiple viewpoints of the killing of Tom and the arrest, trial, and incarceration of Burmah. And a recently discovered transcript shows that the trial was not merely to get justice for the victims but also to heighten the profiles of Los Angeles politicians and the LAPD.

⌇

Tom White is a shadowy figure in this entire story, even though he was responsible for the events that took place in August and September of 1933. One can conclude that he was simply a bad egg, a man who went looking for trouble time and again and found it. Perhaps he was the product of a too-distant military father and an overwhelmed mother. Maybe he had a drinking or drug problem even before he first landed in jail as a teen. Whatever the case, Tom White's life ended the second he pulled a gun on police officers on September 6, 1933—he could never offer any words of explanation for either his deeds or those of his wife.

Today the Los Angeles Public Library houses the *Los Angeles Herald-Examiner*'s photograph collection concerning Burmah White's arrest and trial. The short history that accompanies each one reads, in part: "White's lack of remorse and abrasive demeanor were great fodder for the press, but earned the young widow a guilty conviction on eleven felony counts, and she was sentenced to a term of from 30 years to life. She'd served less than eight years for her part in the 1933 crime spree. Upon her release, White vanished from public view."[12] Burmah's reasons for participating in her crimes were both simple and complicated. Her seeming detachment regarding them is what would alter her life forever.

CHAPTER 1

But Is It Love?

Santa Ana, California, is famous for the dust storms called by its name. They originate in the vicinity and sweep down on Los Angeles, break windows, tear shutters loose, and pour tons of pulverized sand over everything. Crime author Raymond Chandler once wrote that these Santa Anas could "curl your hair and make your nerves jump and your skin itch." The city is located about thirty miles south of Los Angeles, twelve miles inland from the Pacific Ocean, and in the 1920s its center was still surrounded by miles of orange groves. In those early years there were backyard gardens with fruit and nut trees, chickens, and sometimes a cow. There were celery fields near today's Warner and Bristol Streets, and August Reiter's raisin vineyard was where the *Orange County Register*'s newspaper building now stands. Today the homes are citified, and the business area is tightly packed with giant complexes like the Segerstrom Buildings at North Main and Tenth Streets. But in 1925 Santa Ana was spacious, warm, and clean—a perfect respite for someone like Joseph Adams.

Adams contracted tuberculosis in 1920, and like thousands of other Americans, had a doctor who told him to move out West for his health. Reluctant but resigned to the move in hope of getting better, Adams gave up his accountant position in Indianapolis and moved his family to Santa Ana. He already had family in Orange County: a brother and a sister, and an uncle who helped him purchase a delivery service for bakeries. He rented a house on French Street and set out to build a clientele.

Pearlea (she preferred "Pearl"), his wife, was more excited about moving to Southern California. Pearl May Smith was born and raised in Elkhart, Indiana. Her family had suffered one tragedy after another, starting with her younger sister's horrific death in September 1905 when the matches she was playing with caught her dress on fire and continuing with brother Elmer's near-fatal brush with typhoid fever just a few months later. Pearl herself contracted typhoid in 1910 and then suffered scarlet fever in 1911. She recovered and was working as an elementary school teacher when she met Joseph Adams in 1913.

Burmah Arline Adams was born January 9, 1914, in Cleveland, Ohio, where Joseph tried selling insurance for a time. The origin of the name Burmah for girls isn't clear, but it was not uncommon at that time, though it was more prevalent in the South. Her mother and father did not marry for another five years; Joseph had not yet procured a divorce from his first wife, with whom he had a four-year-old son in Kansas. Pearl gave birth to Jo Louraine ten years after Burmah, on March 3, 1924.

In Santa Ana, Burmah, little sister Jo Louraine, and her mother and father moved several times before finding a home on 902 South Birch Street, which was within walking distance of most conveniences and the children's schools. It was on a lovely Magnolia tree–lined avenue surrounded by other working-class families. Pearl set up a home-based business making candied figs and did her best to fill the financial gaps when Joseph's bakery deliveries were few, which became more often the case as the Great Depression gripped the Southland.

Burmah thrived in her new home. Pearl enrolled her in the seventh grade at Julia C. Lathrop Junior High School, where she quickly endeared herself to both teachers and classmates. Administrators noted that although she had skipped second grade back in Indiana and was young for her grade (ten years old), she fully kept pace with her peers scholastically and socially.[1] She participated in piano recitals and made honor roll every semester. The principal chose Burmah's cookbook manuscript for Domestic Science class to be taken by the district superintendent to Honolulu, Hawaii, for a conference that featured grade-school artwork. She was elected an officer in the Every Girl's and Boy's Club; she won awards for typing the fastest on a Remington in vocational class. The lithesome girl was chosen time and again for special dance classes at the YWCA held in conjunction with the school.[2]

Like many children in the late 1920s, Burmah probably could not grasp the magnitude of the struggles her parents and the country at large were having. Businesses and banks throughout the state closed their doors in the 1930s; thousands of individual investors and depositors lost everything. California farm income in 1932 sank to just half of what it had been in 1929. The number of building permits in 1933 was less than one-ninth what it had been eight years earlier. Many property owners lost their farms and their homes. Unemployment in the Golden State reached a staggering 28 percent in 1932; two years later, 20 percent of all Californians were dependent on public relief.[3] And yet millions of refugees from the southern Great Plains states like Oklahoma continued to pour into California to escape even worse conditions, creating "camp cities" up and down the Central Valley, straining the state's tenuous resources.

But near the beaches of Orange County, at Santa Ana High School, Burmah continued to shine. She won a spot in the girls' glee club and attained honor roll status as usual. She could be counted on to join every social event sponsored by the junior society of the First Baptist Church, where her family worshiped. The petite brunette could often be found earning a little extra cash on weekends by serving desserts at wedding receptions—probably cakes her father had delivered.[4]

Burmah's success during this first year of senior high was remarkable considering her bad luck just a few weeks after the start of the year. In the early evening of Friday, September 17, 1926, baseball player Liston Hill turned right on Spurgeon from Washington Street in his car and, not seeing Burmah, knocked her clear off her bicycle. Hill drove the young teen to the hospital, where doctors performed emergency surgery to relieve the pressure building inside her fractured skull. She remained at the Santa Ana Valley hospital for two weeks before doctors allowed her to go home to further recuperate.[5] Her classmates brought her flowers, homework, and puzzles to while away the time until she resumed classes more than a month after the accident.

Years later, when she was on trial, a former teacher of Burmah's blamed her actions on the effects of this accident. "We cannot realize that it is the same Burmah Adams we knew who is involved in this case," said the teacher. "The news of her plight is a terrible blow to the entire faculty at Lathrop. Burmah was a lovely girl when she attended school here. Because of her excellence in scholastic work and sweet personality, we always predicted a wonderful career for her."[6] Teachers told the *Santa Ana Register* that classmates of the defendant remembered that "after her injury Burmah's attitude underwent a change until she finally became a different person from the quiet studious girl of junior high school days."[7]

If there was a change in Burmah's personality—whether from injury, the onset of puberty, or otherwise—it did not prevent her from having friends and performing well in school. Her grades at Santa Ana High were "a great deal more than 'fair,'" according to her former principal, and she excelled at English, Spanish, stenography, and geometry. Her Spanish teacher—Mrs. Trythol—recalled that Burmah was "an unusually intelligent girl" who would never do anything untoward, like cheat on a test. Blanche McDowell lived down the street from the Adamses, and when interviewed years later for one of Burmah's parole applications, she said that Burmah showed unusual kindness toward her father, who was living with a disability. Blanche would often roll Mr. McDowell out onto the front yard for sunshine, and Burmah was one of the few children who would stop and talk to him on the way to school.[8] That kindness was missing during her later career with the son of Thomas White.

❧

Thomas White was born July 21, 1897, in Plattsburgh Barracks Post Hospital in Clinton County, New York, the northernmost county of the state. His father, Thomas White Sr., had emigrated from Manchester, England, in 1882 and enlisted in the US Army almost immediately after his arrival. Plattsburgh was the oldest military installation in America, owing to its strategic location on Lake Champlain. During the colonial era, the lake provided the only method of transportation through the wilderness area of what is now New York state and Vermont; it served as a buffer between American forces and British-Canadian forces during the War of 1812 and later supplied troops who were sent to subdue Seminole Indians and other tribes. In the 1890s the barracks served as a training facility for the 21st Infantry, dubbed the "President's Own" in 1897 because of William McKinley's habit of inspecting the troops while vacationing at the lake.

The senior White was assigned to the 21st Infantry, Company E. While briefly transferred to Fort Omaha, Nebraska, he met a woman named Irene Hamilton, a recent immigrant from Denmark. They married in 1892; he was thirty-one, she seventeen. A daughter, Violet Ellen, was born to the couple while at Fort Omaha, and for the next few years, the family moved back and forth between New York and Nebraska. The 21st Infantry was transferred from Plattsburgh Barracks to Cuba in June 1898 to fight in the Spanish-American War. After the Cuban campaign, the troops returned to Plattsburgh in September 1898.

The children, Tom and Violet, likely could not recall ever living in one place very long. The army moved Thomas and the family from New York, Kansas, Nebraska, Washington State, Wyoming, and Colorado. In December 1899, while in Detroit, Michigan, the Whites welcomed a new baby girl, Maud. In 1900 Irene and the children rented a house near Vancouver Barracks, Washington, where Thomas was stationed.

Tragedy befell the Whites two years later at Fort Russell, Cheyenne, Wyoming. Little Maud developed a vicious case of croup and died in the early morning of June 18, 1902. With military efficiency, the toddler was buried that afternoon at the post cemetery. Within a year, the family moved once again to Fort Leavenworth, Kansas, where the senior White was promoted to the highest enlisted rank available, sergeant major. In 1909, after a short stint at Camp Keithley in the Philippines, White retired from service with honors.[9]

Irene White died in 1909 or 1910. The circumstances are not known, but by the middle of 1910, Violet and Tom were enrolled in Catholic boarding schools in Denver; their father rented a home a few miles away. In April 1911 Tom and a friend were caught stealing bicycles from a grade school; the other boy told authorities they had planned to run away to Mexico. Thomas was committed to the State Industrial School for Boys in Golden, Colorado. Founded on the former site of the State School of Mines, the Industrial School opened in 1881 and was intended to "reform the youth of the State who have become unmanageable at home and disorderly abroad" and to create a humane and progressive rehabilitative school for "incorrigible" youth between the ages of seven and sixteen.[10] For unknown reasons, Thomas was asked to leave the school after sixteen months.

White's first major crime—at least the first one for which he got caught—was attempting to steal from a drugstore in Colorado Springs on August 31, 1916. He and his friend Robert Burton—an accomplished auto thief—pried open a back door and were helping themselves to cash from the register when an off-duty policeman happened by. Officer Steve Armstrong called the police department from a phone box at the street corner, which alerted the thieves, but not in time to escape arrest. White used the alias Frank McDonald, and just before he pleaded guilty in district court a few days later, the Colorado Springs Police Department's brand new Bureau of Identification uncovered his real name. He was sentenced to six months at the Buena Vista Reformatory in Chaffee County.[11]

For the next two years, White cycled in and out of Colorado prisons. His first escape from Buena Vista in 1916 was unremarkable, and sheriffs quickly returned him. In May 1917 he was returned to Buena Vista again for some parole violation and walked off the grounds when a guard was distracted, just months before he would have been set free. About a year later in Colorado Springs, White and two other young men stole a car. Within hours they were found and arrested, and once again he was sent to Buena Vista. Less than a month after arriving at this familiar place, White sawed the bars off the dormitory window of fellow inmate William Hanson. These two plus another inmate fled Buena Vista and made their way west to Salt Lake City, Utah, where White tried to enlist in the army in hope of starting fresh with a new identity.[12]

For reasons unknown, the Utah recruiting office rejected White for service. Desperate, the escapee took a chance by returning to familiar territory near Denver and, using his alias, attempted to sign up for service at Fort Logan. He was nearly successful, but an honorably discharged inmate from Buena Vista also trying to enlist spotted him and alerted military police, who held him until the reformatory's warden took custody of him. Shortly thereafter, White was remanded to the penitentiary in Cañon City because he had turned twenty-one and was no longer eligible for juvenile reform services.

In 1919 White finally finished paying his debt to Colorado society and moved to Los Angeles, where his father and sister now lived at 1406

West Tenth Street. Thomas White Sr., retired at the rank of sergeant major, suffered various stomach ailments from a parasite he had picked up while fighting Muslim Moros in the Philippines in 1907. Violet had a job as a stenographer for a law firm. In July 1920 she married Philip J. Dillon, a mechanic. Tom White got a job as a mechanic at Detroit Electric's Los Angeles branch at 676 Alvarado Street.

Tom made good on his parole terms from Colorado for a few years. But despite the fact that his father and sister were keeping an eye on him, Tom found trouble. The *Los Angeles Times* later noted that he was arrested for drunkenness in October 1924 and later that year for robbery, though the charges did not stick. He was arrested again in March 1927 for a liquor offense of some sort but was acquitted by a jury. His luck ran out on July 30, 1930. A week earlier, he and two conspirators had broken into the M. A. Newmark grocery at 1248 Wholesale Street. They funneled seven hundred dollars' worth of cartons of cigarettes through a delivery chute and tried to sell them to a fence in Hollywood. The men were caught and arrested.[13]

Tom was convicted of grand theft and sentenced to one to ten years. He was imprisoned in San Quentin but transferred to Folsom after he got into an incredibly violent fight with another inmate: White almost succeeded in partially disemboweling his opponent with a homemade shiv of some kind. In return, his antagonist gauged Tom's eye out; it had to be replaced with one made of glass. Still, two years later, prison officials deemed him reformed enough to live in society again. He was released from Folsom in April 1933, paroled into the custody of his sister, Violet.[14] This was two months before he met Burmah Adams.

In 1929 Joseph Adams was really strapped for cash. He worked from early morning until dusk at the bakery, but during the Depression, customers could afford to pay only a fraction of what a loaf of bread cost. In turn, bakeries could afford to pay their truck drivers only enough to cover gasoline and a tiny bit for labor. If one of Joseph's trucks needed repairs, he could count on losing money for that week. Burmah's father started to show the strain of making ends meet, and the stress caused his rheumatism to flare up. In spite of the fact that she wanted to attend college, Burmah dropped out of high school at the beginning of her senior year and instead enrolled in a cosmetology course that was offered for free at the high school. "It seemed the quickest and most practical way to make a living, for, until then, I hadn't been trained to do anything in particular that would fit me for the business world," she said.[15]

Armed with her cosmetology license after six months of training, Burmah quickly found work near her home in Santa Ana, then joined a beauty shop on upscale Balboa Island in the Newport Beach harbor. But she craved more of a social life than these bucolic neighborhoods could offer a young, pretty, and unattached woman, so she took a job on Wilshire Boulevard in Los Angeles and rented an apartment with some other girls. Still, mother Pearl was always dropping in on her, and Burmah felt that if she was to really be "on her own," she must move farther away. When a friend told her about a new beauty shop opening in the heart of San Francisco, Burmah threw caution to the wind and bought a train ticket before her résumé could even arrive there through the mail.

On March 10, 1933, at 5:54 p.m., a 6.4-magnitude earthquake struck the southern part of Los Angeles County. Centered in Long Beach, twenty miles due west of Santa Ana, the temblor killed 127 people throughout the region and leveled buildings for miles. In Burmah's hometown, three people were killed by falling debris: A man and his wife were crushed under toppling bricks outside the Rossmore Hotel, and another man was hit by debris outside the Richelieu Hotel. The city also suffered $150,000 worth of damages to fifty of its major buildings. Although her family was safe, Burmah could not bear the thought of being away from them after such a devastating event; she immediately quit her job in San Francisco and moved back to Los Angeles. She quickly found a job at Mildred Juhnke's beauty parlor on 7715 South Central Avenue.

Burmah found herself spending even more time with her family because her little sister developed a chronic ear infection that required the services of a specialist. Joseph drove Pearl and Jo up to Los Angeles once or twice a week in the battered bakery delivery truck to have Jo's ears drained. They often spent the night in Burmah's apartment at 236 South Coronado Street.

Working in a beauty parlor day after day, Burmah later told *True Story*, a girl is bound to hear a lot of talk. She served all kinds of customers, from hardworking clerks and stenographers to millionaires' wives and sweethearts who, according to Burmah, had more time and money than was good for them. It was only natural, she supposed, that she should admire their beautiful clothes, their diamonds, and their sharp cars. The young cosmetician heard plenty of gossip about interesting dates, swanky hotels and cafés, and the glitter of nightlife. The editor of *True Story* probably elaborated on Burmah's words, but the sentiment was clear: "There's no denying that I began to get the fever to go places and see things. Being a girl, I'd hardly be normal not to want my share of good times, pretty dresses, and masculine attention."[16]

A friend introduced Burmah Adams to Tom White in June 1933. This friend and her date had plans to attend a dinner dance at Sebastian's Cotton Club in Culver City and invited Burmah to accompany them, along with a man they barely knew but referred to as a "good spender." A would-be Cinderella, Burmah rushed through her work the next day, finding it difficult to fix up other women to look their best when she had so much to do herself to get ready for her date. She decided to spend money she did not have on a new dress from Bullock's department store, and it was at this time that she dyed her hair blonde, to bring out the gold flecks in her eyes—not months later to disguise herself, as police later claimed.[17]

It was easy to find nightlife in Los Angeles during Prohibition. Thanks to the proximity of MGM studios, the main drag of Washington Boulevard was the place to be. Sebastian's Cotton Club, at the intersection of Washington and National, was one of the premier jazz clubs in southwestern Los Angeles. Opened in 1926 by Frank Sebastian, the club was one of the first to feature bands of exclusively black musicians. It was open very late and very early. If you made it through the night, you could be served breakfast in the morning. Burmah was dazzled by both Sebastian's and her date that fateful evening: "When the orchestra struck up that dreamy melody, 'Ah, But Is It Love?' and I found myself gliding among all those bewitching lights and shadows, in the arms of Tom

White, some strange new feeling stirred in my heart; something that I'd never felt before." In *True Story* she noted that she felt he was so big and strong with his arms around her. They made a striking couple: Tom slim, about five feet, ten inches tall, with blonde hair and gray eyes; Burmah five feet, one inch tall, with her blonde bob and liquid blue eyes.

Looking back, Burmah recalled that Tom was reluctant to let her dance with her friend's boyfriend. She liked his wanting to keep her to himself. "It gave me a feeling of power," she said, and she hoped this dashing man would ask her for another date. He did ask, or rather he told her he would pick her up at eight o'clock the next night, as though it had already been settled.

For the next four weeks, the couple saw each other nearly every night. "And I was supremely happy," said Burmah, "for he was giving me pleasures I'd never had before; expensive dinners, beautiful flowers, royal entertainment." He always picked her up in fancy new cars, which he would drive as though they were "racing toward death and destruction" up and down a moonlit Pacific Coast Highway. He always had wads of cash in his pockets, and when Burmah timidly noted once or twice that he had a lot of money for someone who seemingly did not work much, he put her at ease. He was, he said with authority, a stock and bond trader, but things were "rather dull" just then. Plus, Tom said, he had recently inherited a lot of money, so he could afford to vacation in style.[18]

Of course White was not a stock and bond trader. He worked as an auto mechanic and chauffeur and occasionally as a welder. These honest jobs, however, did not provide enough money or excitement for the young con. "I wonder why," Pearl Adams lamented later, when her daughter was in prison, "with thousands of girls in Los Angeles, it had to be my daughter's bad luck to meet Tom White."[19]

Chapter 2

Short Romance, Quick Death

Burmah Arline Adams and Thomas N. White married on September 1, 1933. The *Santa Ana Register* called it "one of the prettiest early fall wedding ceremonies" and described all the details of the event, which took place at the Adamses' home:

> *Pompon dahlias, tiny white blooms and ferns banked the fireplace where the ceremony was read at 7:30 o'clock by Judge Chris Pann of Huntington Beach. Decorations throughout the home included large baskets and bouquets of pastel-hued flowers. . . . During the reception which followed, a buffet supper was served from a large table centered with dainty mixed blooms and lighted with pale green tapers in keeping with the pastel decorative theme.*

Burmah wore a formal gown made of black satin and carried a corsage of snowy gardenias. It is highly unlikely that the couple spent their honeymoon weekend on Catalina Island, as reported. The *Register* also printed what Burmah's parents thought to be true at the time, which was that the couple drove up to San Francisco, where Thomas had supposedly just been transferred as a brokerage agent.[1]

After Burmah's arrest, her father, Joseph, always referred to his daughter's nuptials as the "unfortunate wedding." On October 31, 1933, Joseph and wife, Pearl, were called to the stand to discuss the marriage and their concerns about it taking place. The accused teen burst into tears and called out: "Spare them the ordeal of talking about my problems before this crowd! They've been through enough already!"[2] But they were anxious to defend their daughter and to talk of the abuse she suffered at the hands of Thomas White.

According to Joseph's testimony at trial, he first met his daughter's beau on August 20, 1933, at the Coronado Street apartment. The Adams girls and Pearl were all staying there at the time. White was already there when Joseph drove up that morning; Burmah's father noticed that he did not take off his dark sunglasses the entire time he was there. When he finally shamed Tom into taking them off for a moment, Joseph was taken aback by the younger man's staring right eye. It was glass, Tom explained, because he had lost his eye in an auto accident years before. No doubt this put Joseph at ease and probably made him feel a little empathetic, having been through what he had with Burmah and her accident.

A few days later, on the 25th, the young couple came down to Santa Ana together to visit her parents and get their marriage license. Joseph did not see White again until August 31. Defense counsel George Francis asked Joseph if he had noticed any bruises or scars on his daughter's face on or before that day. "I certainly did," he responded, and when prodded for detail, he continued:

> *Well, there was a lump on her forehead . . . and there were several bruises on her arm; and I noticed a bruise up here [showing the jurors with his hands], around her chest. Just how many, I don't remember, but there were several of them and they were not very small, either.*[3]

Moreover, Joseph recalled, he could not help but notice a big black-and-blue bruise on her forehead that did not seem to be fresh but seemed serious enough because it still protruded. And, he said, Burmah had a number of "discolored spots," as well as old and new bruises all over her arms and throat. Of particular concern, he said, was one big bruise on her leg, about four inches in diameter. He confirmed to defense counsel that, yes, he had tried to speak to his daughter about the cause of the bruises, but she would not discuss it with him at all.[4]

Some wedding guests concurred with Joseph's assessment of his daughter's ill-explained bruises (she had told him that some of the bruises were due to falling down the stairs). Defense attorney Francis queried

William Casey, a neighbor of the Adamses, about whether he had noticed any bruises or scars on Burmah at her nuptials. He said he had noticed five or six large black-and-blue marks on her right arm, between her shoulder and elbow. Francis also asked about her demeanor at this time. Casey had known her since she was a little girl and had noticed quite a negative change in her attitude. "Well," he said, "she appeared to be very unhappy for a girl that was about to be married, and under a great mental strain and trying to control herself."[5] William Casey's wife, Silva, was also called to testify to what she had noticed about Burmah on September 1. "There was a large black bruise mark on her right arm," she said, concurring with her husband that it was between her elbow and her shoulder. She also noticed "a large bruised blue place" on her forehead.

Joseph and Pearl Adams had the opportunity later to offer in more detail their impressions of Thomas White and his "courtship" of their daughter. In one of Burmah's applications for parole, not dated but probably in September 1936, they relayed their impressions to the officer, who took detailed notes:

> *After Burmah was introduced to Tom White, he called at the apartment frequently, and in fact, I understood from Mrs. Adams that he and his sister took an apartment upstairs. She said he was not a good looking chap, but was clean and well-dressed looking, and had a moderate amount of money to spend, which he accounted for not only because of his job, but because . . . they had some little money from his estate.*

Pearl Adams told the officer that Thomas made her uncomfortable because he always wore dark sunglasses, and it made him "rather unpleasant" to talk to. She could not see what her daughter saw in this man, and told her so. Moreover, Pearl said, her daughter's physical and mental demeanor changed. She noticed that during the time Burmah was "going with" Tom White, she always seemed to be dazed and was always very pale. She had no idea what they did all day long except work, but they did not seem to stay out late. When Tom White called at the apartment, his deportment and conversation were always all right, and he seemed to say all the right things. After they got engaged, Tom spoke often of when they would have children, giving Pearl the idea that his desire was the normal one of a man who wished to marry and raise a family.[6]

Mrs. Adams placed a measure of blame on Violet Dillon, who—as Thomas's sister—should have told them he was a paroled convict, especially since she was legally in charge of his care.[7] She also noted an incident that happened a few days before the wedding that she had not had the opportunity to tell at trial. When Pearl had gone with Burmah to Thomas and Violet's apartment in south Los Angeles on or about August 27, 1933, to discuss where the wedding should take place, she heard a "great commotion" upstairs; later, when Burmah came downstairs, she had a large lump on her head "and was otherwise abused." Her mother consoled her and said, "Well, you will be a fine bride," to which Burmah replied, upset, "Maybe I won't be a bride." The parole officer must have asked Pearl why she did not do something at this point if it was so obvious that Thomas White was beating her daughter. Pearl told the officer that she had "no thought at the time" of Tom White beating or striking Burmah "because they [the Adams family] had always lived a simple life very far removed from men who struck and beat their womenfolk and that she thought Burmah had simply struck her head."[8] Of course this statement may have reflected denial or naïveté or a need to simply keep her story of Burmah's alleged abuse straight, in case it would help her get parole.

Christopher B. Pann, the justice of the peace from Santa Ana who had married Burmah and Thomas, was called as a prosecution witness during the trial to describe the bride's apparent state of mind when she applied for their license and also days later during the wedding. When prosecution attorney George Stahlman asked if Pann had had any discussions with her about her upcoming marriage, he replied that he did but admitted that White did most of the talking. Stahlman pressed Pann to elaborate on Burmah's attitude during the marriage ceremony.

Attorney Francis vigorously objected, saying that this was calling for a conclusion by the witness. Pann was allowed to answer after Stahlman slightly rephrased the question to ask merely what the justice observed.

PANN: It was in the home of her parents; she greeted me on entrance; seemed natural and normal, pleasant and agreeable.

STAHLMAN: And, after the ceremony was performed, she kissed the groom, did she?

Francis again objected. "I think, your Honor please, there ought to be some bounds of propriety here as far as leading this witness is concerned. . . . He can tell what happened there without counsel putting words into his mouth." He was overruled. Stahlman sharpened his point: "Was there anything about her attitude that indicated to you that she was afraid or sorrowful, or anything of that character?" Pann admitted that he thought the "young lady seemed strained," then added, "I thought she was overly painted or decorated with cosmetics."[9] "Oh," said Stahlman, "you thought she was overly decorated with cosmetics. Quite different than she is at this time?"

This introduction of makeup as fakery was a miscalculation on Stahlman's part. It is likely that George Francis fairly jumped out of his chair to cross-examine Pann:

FRANCIS: Judge, you say you thought she acted strange?

PANN: Slightly strained.

FRANCIS: Strained?

PANN: Strained.

FRANCIS: And in addition to acting slightly strained, why, she was overly painted with cosmetics, as it occurred to you?

PANN: I thought so.

FRANCIS: Yes. Do you recall whether you saw any bruises upon her body or face?

PANN: I did not.

FRANCIS: And was her face so covered with cosmetics that you could not have seen a bruise on her forehead if there had been one there?

Stahlman objected; Francis withdrew the question, but Pann answered anyway: "Oh I couldn't answer that." The court excused the witness.

Pearl Adams later testified that she too had seen pronounced signs of physical abuse of her daughter by Thomas. She saw the same ones on the forehead and the arms and chest but also saw one that was in a more intimate area while her daughter was bathing. "There was a bad bruise right across the pelvic bone, across here," she said, using her hands to show the lowest part of her own midsection. She also saw a mark across Burmah's back, more on her neck, and said she could see that her ankle was injured.

Her mother questioned her repeatedly about her bruises, but Burmah would not discuss them except to give perfunctory answers to stop the conversation. As for the pelvic bruising, the former beautician maintained that she got it on a surfboard. All her explanations of bruises to her mother were lies, Burmah later said. She did not want her mother to worry.

On September 7, Capt. Stanford J. McCaleb of the LAPD's Robbery-Homicide Unit quizzed Burmah in the presence of policewoman Marie Dinuzzo. This was McCaleb's first major crime investigation since he had been reinstated to command the robbery squad just two weeks earlier. The previous May, LAPD chief Roy Steckel removed McCaleb from duty, charging him with "pernicious political activity" and—of all things—"conduct unbecoming an officer" for allegedly allowing the killing of a pet doe while on vacation in Calaveras County, and also allegedly freeing a prisoner who should have been detained. However, in July 1933 City Attorney Ray Chesebro ordered LAPD to reinstate McCaleb immediately, charging that he had been dismissed solely because he would not support then-mayor John Clinton Porter, who was up for reelection against Frank L. Shaw. McCaleb went back to work in the Highland Park division before returning to the West Los Angeles division a few weeks later.[10]

Captain McCaleb asked Burmah if she knew anything about certain robberies, for which he showed her the reports. According to McCaleb, Burmah checked off all the robberies she was affiliated with, stating that she had committed them with Tom White, and also said, "Yes, I got Tom White to commit these robberies because my little sister needed treatment for her ears, and I committed the robberies with Tom to get money to pay for those treatments."[11] When the prosecution attorney asked McCaleb about Burmah's seeming state of mind when she said that, he strenuously maintained that she was *not* confused or dazed.

Defense counsel Francis did not agree. On cross, he asked McCaleb if he had not given a statement to the press right after interrogating Burmah:

> *And you told those newspaper reporters that she had not told you everything, that she was on the dope and when she got off of the dope and her mind cleared up she would ask for more dope and you would probably be able to get all the information out of her, did you not?*

McCaleb finally admitted that he did say this to reporters but that he said it on September 6, not the 7th. "She appeared to be full of hop, did she?" asked Francis. The captain agreed that she did, but on the 7th she appeared normal.

If one of Burmah's own accounts of her ordeal are to be believed, she did have some experience with drugs while in her relationship with White.[12] After Tom shot Allen and Withington, she recounted, her "nervous tension" gave way to hysteria when they were safe inside their apartment. White went upstairs and returned with a bottle of liquor. "Here," he said, "this will fix you up." Burmah swallowed it, experiencing "an acrid, sweetish something that must have been very powerful" because she immediately felt drowsy and fell asleep a minute later. When she got hold of a newspaper the next day and saw what they had done to Cora Withington especially, she purportedly flopped into a chair and sobbed, "Oh, Tom, how could you?" Her soon-to-be husband's response was, "All you need, my girl, is a good stiff bracer. . . . You'll have to have some courage put into you," and he got her a glass of wine. This time, instead of

17

making her fall asleep, the drink made her extra alert, keener of mind. "I felt elated without reason, and things didn't look so ominous and forbidding as they had at first." Burmah told the writer that White would never let her see him pour her drinks, and she felt lucky to avoid addiction, owing to the fact that this "whirl of crime" she was involved with covered only twenty days.[13]

The last day of that whirl was supposed to be the day Burmah and Thomas were to move to San Francisco, where ostensibly he was to start his job as a stockbroker. Despite the fact that he had no job waiting for him and no discernible skills for legitimate work besides those of a mechanic, Burmah felt some measure of relief that they would be moving to a city she knew—where she could get work and where her husband might leave his violent tendencies behind. Certainly they would be far removed from the crimes they had committed and less likely to be connected with them. Most importantly, Burmah's parents would not be close enough to quiz her about things that did not seem to add up.

Burmah later told *True Story* magazine and various newspapers that she thought Tom was rather moody and quiet, but she was intrigued by his silence. "I mistook it for deep feeling governed by great self-control." In fact, he was so reserved at times that Burmah thought he might not care about her as much as he said he did. "I'd try making him jealous," she plotted. She called a young man she knew from high school, Al, who she knew was infatuated with her. "I gave him what little encouragement he needed," Burmah recalled, "and it was agreed that the next time he came to Los Angeles, he was to come see me." And the gentleman did, on the evening of August 16, the same day that Burmah and Tom had held up and shot Cora Withington and Crombie Allen. Tom had recently taken a room in the same building as Burmah, "probably so he could keep a better watch over me." Al had to leave early, so Burmah took care to leave her table set for two and her date's cigar prominently displayed in the ashtray. "Yes, of course I've had company," the teen said when Tom angrily observed the remains of their dinner. "And why not? I have a right to. We're not engaged!" According to Burmah, Tom's face turned a "sickly gray," and he swore one terrible oath after another and then said, "I'll fix you, young lady, so that you'll never want to see any of your 'nice friends' again, as long as you live! You think I've got a lot of dough, don't you? Think I'm rich? Think I've got a gold mine? Well, I *have*—and here it is!" He purportedly whipped out of his pocket the revolver that he used in many of the duo's crimes and waved it around in her face.[14] Burmah's familiarity with the weapon would be recounted in detail in her trial in just two short months from this episode.

It is true that Thomas kept a close eye on his bride. On the afternoon of September 6, he sent her down to the auto garage, which was about a block from their apartment on 236 South Coronado Street. Here Burmah was to retrieve their car, which was really the coupe they had stolen from Leslie Bartel and which needed a few repairs in order to make the 300-mile trek to San Francisco. The alley from their apartment to the garage was an L shape, so Tom was able to wait around the corner from it, out of sight, while his wife went to pay the bill and get some gas.

As Burmah approached the garage, she noticed several men in greasy overalls hanging around. They did not seem to be paying attention to her, though, so she thought little of it. She drove the auto to the bend in the alley, where her husband hopped in, and they drove back to the private garage a few doors down from the apartment. Suddenly, the engine faltered, and Burmah almost backed into a car coming up behind. The driver swore at her and asked what the hell she was doing. She did "exactly what he wanted me to," she recalled later, which was to turn around and stare at the angry driver, giving him a good look at her face. "I recognized him as one of the men I'd seen at the garage," she said, "but I didn't know until later that he was a police officer in disguise."[15]

Burmah put the car away at their apartment building—the Casa del Monte—and Tom ran upstairs while she dropped into her old apartment, number 18 on the third floor, where her mother and Jo resided. The family spoke for a minute or two before one of the men in greasy overalls burst through the front door. "Where's your boyfriend?" the man demanded. "He's upstairs, I guess," replied Burmah. The man began to pepper her with questions about the holdups of the previous weeks, and she hastily went over close to him and begged him quietly not to question her any more just then. "I'll tell you anything later," she said, "only I don't want my mother to know." "Well, all right," replied the man. "But she'll have to know it sooner or later." Burmah choked back tears. She wanted time to think, to think about how to tell her mother gently of her involvement in all of these crimes.[16]

But there would be no time to think because she heard a scuffle in the hallway outside her door then three pistol shots. Burmah heard a deep voice call out, "We got him!" The mechanic/officer with her opened the door and looked out; two other officers pushed into the apartment and said the bride would have to go with them. "Miss," one of them suggested apologetically, "maybe you'd better not go out this way. His body is lying right here, blocking the way." "Never mind," Burmah replied, "I'll step over him."[17] This she did, before trying to hurl herself through the third-story window. One of the policemen seized her and placed her in handcuffs. "Where is the Chevrolet?" Officer William Chester Burris asked Burmah, rifling through her leather purse. "I haven't any Chevrolet," she responded, according to the report Burris typed later. "I just saw you drive away from the filling station with it," Burris said. "What did you do with it?" She replied, "You ought to know."[18]

Besides the keys to the Chevrolet, the policemen found some other things in Burmah's purse and apartment. There was a driver's license that belonged to a Laura Freericks in her bag and some unidentified items that belonged to three men who were found in Tom White's upstairs apartment. These men were Ova McConville, Walter Cooper, and James Russell, who were arrested as "asserted associates of White." LAPD then arrested William A. Freericks and his wife, Laura, who lived in another apartment building a couple of miles away.[19] Neither the *LA Times* nor any other paper nor the trial ever discussed the three men and the Freerickses again after brief mentions the first two days after Burmah was arrested; the arrestees were handed over to the Federal Bureau of Investigation. The implications of these arrests as they pertained to Burmah White would not fully develop for another couple of years, and they would never become known to the general public.

Burmah's utterances, especially the ones she made about stepping over the body of her husband, and her questions ("Is he dead? Is he dead?") before trying to jump out the window cost her dearly in the court of public opinion. As reported in the press, they gave the impression of a cold, indifferent soul who had no empathy or sympathy for another human being and, worse, the impression that she had committed crimes with her husband without any emotional attachment to him—therefore, for no reason at all. This indifference was also intimated a couple of days later by the caption underneath a *Herald-Examiner* photo of Burmah looking at her husband's corpse: "She haughtily walked into the morgue and posed with icy indifference, then like an actress going into a 'sob scene' she managed to sniffle a bit."[20]

But in her version of events in *True Story*, the bride explains why she sounded so heartless and unfeeling. At that moment, she said, "I *was* unfeeling. I had, for the moment, 'gone dead.' Every emotion in me was frozen up." When she said she'd step over Tom White's body, "I hardly knew what I was saying, or what I felt. I can't say that I was glad he was dead. I wouldn't want to be guilty—consciously—of such a thought about anybody. Life is too precious. And yet, as I glanced at his motionless body, prone on the floor where it had toppled from the stairs above, a voice seemed to whisper to me, 'Now you are free! Even if you go to prison, you are freer than you would ever have been with him.'"[21]

A week after the shootout with Tom White and the arrest of Burmah, Mayor Frank Shaw held a ceremony at the city hall for the six police officers involved: A. J. Bergeron, B. G. Anderson, W. C. Burris, Harry R. Maxwell, and two radio officers. Chief James Davis and Martin Neuner, president of the police commission, gave them letters of commendation. The ceremony took place right after the city council formally adopted the felon registration ordinance as part of the officials' anti-gangster campaign.[22]

Chapter 3

Pretrial

From her cell in Los Angeles County Jail, Burmah wrote an open letter to young women and gave it to her lawyers for the *Los Angeles Herald and Express* to print. The cautionary tale is crafted in her loopy, feminine, and neat handwriting:

> *Crime never pays!*
>
> *In the freedom and laxity of this modern day and age, the general tendency of girls in their late 'teens and early twenties to accept people at their face value, without questioning, is drastically wrong.*
>
> *Girls, before furthering any acquaintance with a prospective suitor, make sure you know who he is, where he is from, and who his family is. In other words, investigate him thoroughly first!*
>
> *Perhaps, had I more thoroughly delved into the life of Tom White, I would never have found myself in the position I do today. Broken, dejected, humiliated, and ostracized!*
>
> *Let my bitter experience be a lesson to you.*
>
> *Burmah A. White[1]*

That she might soon be writing a letter from a jail cell was the last thing on Burmah's mind as detective lieutenants W. C. Burris and Harry Maxwell gripped her in her third-story bedroom window while police swarmed around the body of Thomas White in the hallway. Burris then handed Burmah over to Maxwell and started searching her bedroom. Within a minute he found a dark brown men's suit like the one described as being worn by Thomas when he held up his victims. He also found a "turban hat," just as the victims described as being part of the woman's attire.[2] Burmah was taken to the city jail in Lincoln Heights, where she was met by Donald MacKay, a public defender, who advised her immediately not to speak to anybody about anything. Before Burmah was led to her cell, Captain McCaleb attempted to question her, but she said few words: "You'll have to prove me guilty," she told her interrogators with a "steady smile," and responded to all others with "I don't know," or "I can't say," or "I couldn't tell you." According to the *Times*, Burmah smiled during this questioning except for a brief moment when she cried a bit then "went on smiling again."[3] Finally, McCaleb handed his charge over to policewoman Marie Dinuzzo and told a gathering of newspaper reporters that Mrs. White would "tell the truth when her smile wears off."[4]

There is contrasting evidence about Burmah's physical condition during her incarceration in the Lincoln Heights jail. Personnel may have been following simple procedure, or MacKay may have insisted that they check to see if she had any bruises or cuts or evidence of using drugs at the time she was arrested so that he could weave that into his defense. Emily D. Latham, secretary of the Board of Prison Trustees for the State of California, did some investigation into this matter later while compiling evidence of whether Burmah should be paroled. The correspondence stating this evidence is not dated but was probably typed in 1935 or 1936 after one of White's parole applications. The secretary drove to Highland Park, an artsy section of northeast Los Angeles adjacent to Pasadena. She interviewed Rose Pickerel, a policewoman who had charge of the women prisoners at the Lincoln Heights jail and was responsible for Burmah when she was arrested. Pickerel, noted Latham, said Burmah was kept "incommunicado" during the first few days of her incarceration, before she was transferred to county jail. Latham asked if this inmate had any marks of abuse, such as beatings, on her body; Pickerel said there were not. She also said that they would have been discovered if there had been, as Burmah was given a very thorough physical examination to see whether she had been taking drugs. She added that it was the staff's impression at first that Burmah had been "taking dope" because she "acted in a dazed manner," but that no evidence was found of it. Furthermore, Pickerel said, Burmah needed "no medical attention" of any kind and showed "no sorrow over her husband's death, did not cry, and it was her opinion that she did not care for him."[5]

Pickerel did not participate in Burmah's trial, but policewoman Dinuzzo did. Dinuzzo testified that the teen had only a "slight bruise on the right arm." The prosecuting attorney asked her to clarify: Had she removed all of Burmah's clothing? She had; she had checked the prisoner's entire body, and that was the only bruise she saw. "Did you see any bruise on her pelvic bone?" None whatever, she responded. "Did you see any bruise on her back?" No, Dinuzzo said. But just moments later, the prosecution asked its witness whether she remembered that Burmah told her she received a bruise on her head and arm by falling down some stairs. Dinuzzo said yes; in fact, Burmah told her that was how she obtained those bruises. The defense attorney immediately caught the significance of this and finally got Dinuzzo to admit that she had seen a bruise on Burmah's forehead when the latter was arrested.[6]

But Pearl Adams later testified to a parole investigator—perhaps to Latham herself—that at the time of the trial, the matron who had received Burmah at the Lincoln Heights jail upon her arrest was not available to testify because she was on vacation. If she had been there, said Mrs. Adams, "she could have testified that Burmah's body was badly bruised from beatings"; furthermore, Mrs. Adams spoke "many times of Burmah's dazed manner and extraordinarily white face during this period." The parole interviewer asked Burmah's mother if she thought Burmah might be taking drugs, and she responded that to her knowledge she did not and "that she did not believe that Burmah knew what drugs were; that it might be that Tom White had given them to her, but if he had, that was her first experience with them."[7]

A Santa Ana newspaper dug a little more deeply into the drug rumors surrounding Burmah: "While police are endeavoring to prove Burmah White a hardened criminal and narcotic addict, former acquaintances in Santa Ana are recalling the girl and her change from a studious school child to a girl who 'went places and did things.'" This unnamed source insisted that Burmah was never the same after being hit by the car and that from the time of her "apparent recovery" Burmah Adams was a different girl altogether:

From a quiet, studious girl Burmah was transformed to a "stepper," it was said. Quitting high school, she worked for a time behind the fountain in drug stores. Later she attended "beauty school" and upon graduation was employed in a beauty parlor. It was while working there that she first changed the color of her hair. From then on she alternated between her natural dark hair through the various shades of blonde.

When she first acquired her drug habit is unknown. That she is a drug addict is the claim of Capt. Eddie Chitwood of the Los Angeles Police narcotic squad. Her addiction to narcotics, he said, included an addiction to cocaine, which, he said, was clearly indicated by her physical condition.[8]

Captain Chitwood explained that he and policewoman Marie Dinuzzo gave Burmah a thorough examination upon her arrest and that they found the inner nasal membranes raw and inflamed. This, he said, was a typical symptom of cocaine users. "I see you are on the junk," Chitwood said to Burmah, according to his recollection. Burmah denied this, saying she "did not know whether the drug was a liquid or a powder." Chitwood then darkened her eyes—the paper did not say how he did this—and freed them to look at a lighted match. Her pupils did not contract like a normal person's, he said. Chitwood did not take part in Burmah White's trial.

The deputy district attorney assigned to Burmah's case, Donald MacKay, was born in Marquette, Michigan. MacKay moved to Los Angeles with his parents and brother when he was eleven years old, in 1903. He attended Polytechnic High School on West Washington Street in the heart of the city. He spent several years as a carpenter and seven as a Los Angeles police officer before deciding to become a lawyer. He graduated from the College of Law of the University of Southern California in 1923 then served as deputy district attorney of Los Angeles County from 1924 until 1928, eventually rising to chief trial deputy district attorney. In 1928 MacKay went into private practice with his brother, Olin.

In many ways, MacKay was more colorful than some of his clients. He left his first wife when he fell in love with the woman who would become his second, a client who had been busted for making and distributing bathtub gin. One of his favorite pastimes was writing poetry, and much to the chagrin of both his first and second wives, he often took payment in goods rather than cash if a client could not afford to pay. MacKay's granddaughter still has one of the paintings given to him as payment hanging in her home as a reminder of the ancestor who fought for the underdogs of Los Angeles. In 1929 a Los Angeles Superior Court jury found MacKay not guilty on charges of accepting a $7,500 bribe from an auto magnate to steer a case in the latter's favor. Olin was implicated as a middleman in his brother's alleged scheme but was not charged.[9] In 1937, however, Olin was permanently disbarred for portraying a client as an attorney with no flight risk when in reality the man was a convicted felon.

On the evening of September 8, 1933, Burmah was led to the "shadowbox" room at LAPD headquarters. There she was told to stand on a stage of sorts along with her sister-in-law. It is not clear why Violet, who was not being charged with any crime, would stand with Burmah; she may have insisted on doing so to provide support. Witnesses and victims of Thomas and Burmah's crimes stood below and back from the platform and in front of searing klieg lights, which allowed them to see Burmah but not the other way around. The *Los Angeles Evening Herald and Express* took a photo of the procedure and printed it the next day with some colorful description: "With a sneering smile on her face, 19-year-old Burmah Adams White, icy blonde bride of the slain 'rattlesnake' bandit, is pictured as she appeared in the glaring spotlight of the police shadowbox last night for identification by the bandit's victims. The victims are silhouetted in the shadows as they gaze at the defiant blonde, standing between Detective Lieutenants W. C. Burris, left, and Harry Maxwell."[10]

William Chester Burris's first memories were those of running through orange tree groves in the city of Pomona. His father picked fruit there in the early 1900s, having fled the biting cold winters and poverty of Moultrie County, Illinois, to start a family in balmy Southern California. The elder Burris learned the intricacies of irrigation in this burgeoning agricultural region and moved his family around various hamlets between the Inland Empire and San Gabriel Valley. Like nearly every other able-bodied young man, Chester left home in 1917 to fight in World War I. Upon his return, the younger Burris worked with his father in the busy but bucolic citrus region of his youth, but he longed for something more exciting.

On the afternoon of December 29, 1921, Chester's father went to go fix a loose board at the water pumphouse of the ranch that he managed, and where the family lived. He took a quarter-inch length of iron pipe and carefully tried to dislodge the board, mindful that he was just a few feet from the transformer. But because there was more moisture in the air than usual, a charge jumped from the transformer, traveled through the pipe and sent fifteen thousand volts of electricity through the elder Burris, hurling him back ten feet. Chester, home from his job in Los Angeles for the Christmas holiday, heard the explosion from their residence and found his father at death's door near the water station.

While other workers looked on, terrified and mesmerized, Burris began to work over his father's inanimate form. As an assistant medic in the army, the younger man had learned forms of artificial respiration and set to work using them. He threw his father's arms back and forth above his head, blew into his nostrils, and slapped and kneaded his chest any number of ways to try to produce circulation. Ten long minutes later, the injured man gasped and began to breathe on his own. The elder Burris was badly burned, but he went on to live a long and prosperous life.

When reporters interviewed friends and family about Chester's incredible feat, they quickly found out it was not the first time he had saved a life in this manner—he had seemingly brought a fellow soldier back from death in a flu ward during the war, after another medic had given up and slid a sheet over the man's head. But it was his father's ordeal that spurred Chester to quit his job at a furniture store and devote his life to helping others. He joined the LAPD in 1922.

Harry Richard Maxwell also served in the military during the Great War, albeit in the National Guard. He received an honorable discharge in spring 1919 and joined the LAPD in 1921. In 1925 Maxwell was removed from duty while the LAPD investigated charges that he had extorted a druggist for one hundred dollars to look the other way for a Prohibition violation. Stocky but fit, with sharply defined features and a cleft chin, piercing blue eyes set closely against the nose, and a gravelly voice, this Ohio native could be especially formidable with accused criminals.

Three days after the shooting, on September 9, Burmah was led from her cell by two policewomen and driven to the Hall of Justice at Temple and First Streets to attend the coroner's inquest of her dead husband. She sat in the front row of Deputy Coroner Frank Montfort's jury room, with a policeman on each side of her. Throngs of people who could not fit into the hall pressed their faces against the windows in an effort to get a glimpse of the proceedings. Detective Bergeron, who related details about the stakeout and attempt to get White to surrender, followed Violet. Mrs. White—Burmah—was called to the stand "for the purpose of identification" but refused to speak, on advice of counsel MacKay. According to the *LA Times* reporter covering the event, she smiled once or twice as witnesses identified her as the criminal companion of Thomas White, though at other times, her "unnaturally curly hair" shook with nervousness as victims discussed their ordeals.

Several policemen involved in White's shooting and the victims made their positive identifications, including Crombie Allen, who remarked, "Yes, that is the man. It serves him right."[11] Montfort submitted his medical findings to a jury of nine, which ultimately ruled the shooting of Thomas White a "justifiable homicide." Violet Dillon fell to the floor sobbing when she saw her brother laid out motionless on the coroner's table.

Photographers crowded into the little anteroom at Edwards Brothers Mortuary near downtown Los Angeles, where the body lay. They jostled for the best position to take pictures of Tom White's family and the victims of his crimes. After the inquest was finished, the funeral home held a short service for family, which consisted of Violet Dillon and Burmah White sitting awkwardly next to each other in the pews, with policemen surrounding both of them. In the midst of the service, Lieutenant Burris lost his temper with photographers using flashbulbs and muscled them out of the parlor. The shutterbugs later filed suit with Buron Fitts, but Fitts refused to prosecute or reprimand Burris and in fact wrote a letter of commendation about his actions to Chief Davis. "It does seem to me," Fitts wrote, "that at some stage of a person's life, they should be entitled to some decent privacy, and most certainly one of those times ought to be during funeral services." It isn't clear whether Fitts was referring to Burmah, Violet, Tom, or all of them, but his feelings were clear: This situation was so sad and peculiar all the way around that he felt the family had at least earned a tiny bit of dignity.[12]

Burmah was twice allowed to go in the anteroom and view her husband's body. The first time, she stared at him, emotionless. On the way to see him a second time, she burst into tears, providing some much-wanted drama for onlookers who were lucky enough to get a seat in the room.[13] The next day, officials transferred Burmah to the county jail.

<hr>

On September 29, 1918, four years before he became Los Angeles district attorney, Buron Rogers Fitts lay dying on a dark field in northeastern France. A German explosive had struck his right knee; stretcher bearers could not reach him for several hours, during which time he almost bled to death. But after fourteen months in the hospital, where he was also treated for mustard gas burns, Fitts was able to return home to California and practice law.

Fitts's parents had moved to Los Angeles in 1905, two years after Donald MacKay did. He also graduated from the University of Southern California's law school and clerked for famed defense attorney Earl Rogers. A year after he was admitted to the state bar in 1916, he enlisted in the US Army. Although he returned a hero, lingering effects of his knee wound would, over the years, require him to undergo more than twenty operations and eventually have the limb amputated. In 1920 he became commander of the California branch of the American Legion and two years later headed the California Veterans' Bond campaign to enhance benefits for returned soldiers. In addition to his American Legion activities, Fitts joined the district attorney's staff and rose rapidly through the ranks.[14]

Fitts was a man who, as *LA Times* historian Cecilia Rasmussen describes, fought crime and his political opponents with the same bare knuckles. "Throughout his three-term career, he raised the rate of successful prosecutions from 55 percent to 82 percent in Los Angeles County, and gained a measure of fame for the speed with which cases were processed."[15]

As Los Angeles crime historian Don Wolfe aptly put it, "Buron Fitts had covered up enough crimes and scandals to decimate forests of tabloid pulp." One of his more famous concealments was the alleged suicide of Paul Bern, husband of actress Jean Harlow. On September 5, 1932, Bern was found naked and shot in the head at the couple's Beverly Hills home; a coroner's jury concluded that it was a suicide. A year later, however, about the time of Burmah's tribulations, a county grand jury was taking a hard look at Fitts's finances, prompted by information from confidential informants that he had been bribed by MGM Studios to cover up Bern's murder by a deranged common-law wife—the studio's morals clause frowned on bigamy more than suicide. In 1929, as he sat on the opposite side of the courtroom from attorney Jerry "Get Me" Giesler, who was defending theater magnate Alexander Pantages against statutory rape charges, Fitts could not have imagined that he too would soon retain the famed defense lawyer—again, for taking a bribe from a defendant.[16]

In November 1930, after two attempts at prosecution with scant evidence of wrongdoing, Fitts was forced to drop charges against a trial attorney accused of taking a bribe. The accused lawyer was none other than Donald MacKay.[17]

Fitts was tough—by the end of his career, he had survived three gunshot wounds, more than twenty operations, a grand jury indictment and trial for bribery, and the scandalous revelations in a prostitute's little black book.[18] His penchant for celebrity friends often caused quite a stir, as when he sent his most handsome deputy to Union Station with orders to give the arriving Mae West a big kiss, saying, "This is from Buron." Her reply has entered legend: "Is that a gun in your pocket, or are you just glad to see me?"[19]

After serving as a deputy district attorney in Los Angeles for six years, Fitts took leave and successfully ran for lieutenant governor in 1926. Two years after that, when his former boss, Los Angeles District Attorney Asa Keyes, was indicted for bribery in the Julian Petroleum swindle—one of the earliest and largest Ponzi schemes in US history—Fitts was elected in his place. Old loyalties, however, did not prevent him from quickly winning a conviction of Keyes.[20]

The scandals surrounding the Keyes administration combined with Fitts's personal prestige and widespread press support to generate a mandate to "clean house." Within a week, Fitts began to reorganize operations.

He introduced a new Bureau of Investigation, modeled after the FBI. This staff of sixty to seventy men gave Fitts his own force of detectives, independent of either the Los Angeles police or sheriff's departments, and a fruitful source of patronage for his political allies and American Legion confederates.[21]

On September 11, 1933, with his usual speediness, Fitts announced that a grand jury would convene the next day to consider the charges against Burmah Adams White. He and his team planned to present evidence in fifteen robbery counts against her. The *Times* noted that MacKay was "undecided as to his client's course, but strongly intimated she will continue her silence even when faced with trial"; however, he would offer a defense to the "apparently iron-clad case" of the prosecution.[22] Before proceedings started on the 12th, Burmah was allowed to attend the funeral of her slain husband, which the *Times* noted she left "dry-eyed" and irritated: "Just a farce, that funeral," she said. "There were only a couple of sob sisters for an audience, and they didn't even know Tom." She wondered out loud why the county did not "just take care of it," referring to the cost of the funeral, which the city must have been charged to her family instead of taxpayers as it did for victims of homicide.[23]

Burmah confessed to the grand jury that she was White's accomplice in all the crimes of which she was accused. The *Times* ran a photo of her appearing to smile coyly as she sat next to grand jury foreman Dr. William A. Griffith. She spoke of meeting Thomas at a "dinner dance" just two and a half months prior and more recently driving up to victims and waiting while he told them to hand over their valuables, not knowing exactly what he was saying. "There," she said, while leaving the jury room, "that will probably mean ten or fifteen years for me but I'll stand up and take it on the chin."[24]

But Burmah also detailed why all her activities were not entirely her fault. She was a victim of Thomas's also, she said, offering a half apology to Crombie Allen: "I'm awfully sorry that it happened," she said, "but you must realize I had no control over him." During her testimony, she spoke of falling in love with White immediately and of how he presented himself as a businessman and an heir to family money—not realizing he was neither until it was too late and he made her participate in the

Allen-Withington robbery-shooting. After that, she explained, he forced her to marry him so she could not testify against him. She could not simply leave him, Burmah continued, because he threatened her with more beatings and death if she did. "We're both in it now," White allegedly said after reading about the Allen-Withington affair. "If you ever open your trap you'll get the same thing."[25]

Out of a city of nearly a million and a half souls, Burmah and Tom White shot two people highly connected to the media, Cora Belle Withington and Crombie Allen. Setting aside the fact that Allen was a newspaper owner and editor for a media empire in a county next to Los Angeles, he was extremely active in his community and loved by many. He gave USC's journalism department large amounts of scholarship money for promising undergraduates; he was former president of (and still active with) the California Newspaper Publishers association, a Rotary Club office holder and speaker, an ambassador for bringing the Summer Olympics to Los Angeles in 1932, and a world traveler who was often asked to advise California lawmakers.

Allen was widowed with a small daughter and was in no hurry to replace little Jane's mother. But mutual friends had discovered that he and Cora Withington were both transplants from suburbs of Pittsburgh, Pennsylvania, and urged them to meet. For her part, Cora was not looking to start a family—the time for that had passed, and she was very busy with her career as a teacher. Withington came to California armed with a degree from the renowned Indiana State Teacher's College and was a first grade instructor at Third Street School in the upscale Hancock Park neighborhood. Her students were the children of prominent bankers, lawyers, politicians, and doctors. The students' mothers were wives of those prominent professionals and made up a volunteer force to be reckoned with, by way of the parent teacher association. They worked closely with Withington, who spearheaded an arts program for the young minds of the school.

One of these mothers was Elsie Moody, wife of physician Egbert Earl Moody. All three Moody children went to Third Street, as did Elsie's brother's children, in part because of Withington's progressive teaching. Elsie grew up a few homes away from Harrison Gray Otis, manager of the

Times-Mirror Company, which owned the *Los Angeles Times*. After Otis's death in 1917, Elsie's parents and then she and her husband remained close friends with Harry Chandler, who succeeded his father-in-law as president and publisher of the *Times*.[26] Harry Chandler was also a principal in what historians have dubbed "the Combination": a short-lived but formidable gentlemen's agreement between the *LA Times*, Fitts, Davis, Mayor Frank Shaw, and mafia attorney Kent Parrot, whereby the *Times* would launch no anti-vice crusades and Parrot would not interfere with the LAPD's anti-union "Red Squad." Parrot and Davis would do what they could to help Chandler create the illusion of Los Angeles as the "Great White Spot," a city free of crime and communism; this meant intense crackdowns on lower-level thugs and criminals who curried no favor with City Hall or the LAPD. The Combination began cooperating in earnest in July 1933, when Frank Shaw was elected mayor. In Shaw's first campaign for mayor, the *Los Angeles Times* questioned his qualifications, even calling into question his citizenship (he was Canadian born). After Shaw won office, however, he seemed to win the *Times* over by reappointing a favorite of theirs to be police chief: James Davis.

Burmah Adams White was indicted on seven counts of robbery, three of assault with a deadly weapon and intent to commit murder, and one of attempted robbery. Her bail was set at twenty-five thousand dollars, an amount she would not be able to raise even partially under any circumstances. The "blonde bandit" was led to county jail to await her trial, which was set for October 21, 1933—a mere twenty-four days later. Somehow, the *Los Angeles Evening Herald and Express* got possession of a note Burmah wrote in September 1933—exactly what day or to whom is not known. But she was most certainly speaking of her upcoming trial when she wrote, "I am gambling for high stakes; either I win in a big way or lose in an equally large way."[27]

CHAPTER 4

Pop Culture

"Where are we gonna get a car?" asked the sultry Burmah. "We're gonna have to stick up people in the street!"

"Oh, that's small time stuff," Tom replied. "We're gonna operate in a *big* way."

"Yeah, but where are we gonna get a car?"

"You see that car stoppin' right there? That's technically ours right now."

"You mean . . . you're gonna take it from 'em?"

"Sure."

"Gee, you're a hard guy, Tom!"

"Sure I am, baby. How 'bout you? You scared?"

"Me scared? Nooo. I get a kick out of it!"

So went the first couple of minutes of "The Burmah White Case" on the December 6, 1933, broadcast of the radio program *Calling All Cars.* The episode segued into a re-creation of the night of August 16, when "every shortwave set from Burbank to Laguna Beach, a distance of seventy-five miles, picked up the breathless message: 'Calling Car Seventeen! Seventeen, go to Occidental, near Third! Auto robbery with violence and an ambulance follow up. That is all!'" As the alarm broadcast died away, the shrill scream of a siren sounded south of Wilshire Boulevard. Car 17 was on its way in response to a telephone call to Los Angeles Police Headquarters by a somewhat hysterical young salesman. Many in Los Angeles knew what had happened between the Whites and Crombie Allen and Cora Withington almost as soon as the police did, for in that "free and easy metropolis," police radio signals were not coded or keyed.[1]

Writer Frederick Lindsley used these true events as background in his script for *Calling All Cars*, which was sponsored by the Rio Grande Oil Company and which originated on the West Coast over the Columbia Broadcasting System. It was the only radio show to use real dispatchers from the LAPD. Like all the episodes did, this one featured a dramatization of a true crime story, how the crime was solved, and how justice was served. This episode was aptly called "The Burmah White Case," or, as it was called in a magazine supplement to the show, "The Circle of Death," presumably a reference to Tom White's demise.[2] Although another episode aired November 29, 1933, it was "a practice run"—a shorter, experimental one to see if the format worked. It did, and "The Burmah White Case" was the program's first full-length episode to air.

Cars had plenty of material to work with. After all, just a few weeks before "The Burmah White Case" aired, its nineteen-year-old namesake was convicted of eleven counts of robbery and assault and sentenced to thirty years to life in prison. Two victims of crimes committed by her and her husband, Thomas White, each lay in their homes recovering from bullet wounds inflicted by White. Crombie Allen talked very slowly and carefully to his friends and family so as not to disturb the stitches on his neck from the slug that had shredded its left side. He would fully recover in a couple of months. Cora Withington was not as lucky. The bullet from the .32-20 caliber revolver that hit Allen had been tempered by first tearing through Withington's left temple and bursting out next to her right eye, destroying her optic nerves and blinding her for life. She was not married, had no family in Los Angeles, and would not be able to continue the job as a third-grade teacher that she had cherished for thirty years. Withington spent the holidays in agony and in the dark in her South Rampart Boulevard apartment. And yet she was grateful to be alive, which she was solely because Allen managed to not pass out from his own wound while driving her to St. Vincent's hospital that night.

There were many, many other victims of violence that summer of 1933 in Los Angeles. That year, the nationwide homicide mortality rate hit a high for the century up to that point—about 10 per 100,000 people—largely attributed to the poverty created by the Great Depression and the black-market violence associated with Prohibition. In July alone there were twenty-four homicides in the county of Los Angeles, fifteen in the city. From July 1, 1932, to June 30, 1933—the police fiscal year—10,154 burglary reports and 2,409 robbery reports were filed. In almost every robbery, the victim had been made to stand and deliver by a bandit armed with a deadly weapon. Under the separate classification of "grand theft" came 738 reports, and 7,920 automobiles were stolen from the city streets. For these reasons, the LAPD was eminently concerned with the "inscrutable riddle of gangdom" that plagued its own metropolis.[3]

In fact, in the late 1920s and early 1930s civilians and police in Los Angeles were convinced that the Golden State was importing crime from other states. Setting aside the much-studied racism and blockades against Mexicans and Dust Bowl migrants, the city did have reasonable fear of gang violence taking over its streets. Benjamin "Bugsy" Siegel and Meyer Lansky would not relocate to California for a few more years, but their predecessors—Italian street gangs like the Matranga, Ardizzone, Dragna, and Roselli families—had controlled liquor-smuggling, gambling, and loan rackets for decades by the time Burmah's trial came to pass in 1933. A generation of politicians and LAPD officers and sheriff deputies for the county remembered the warnings they were given by their East Coast brethren at the start of their careers: "A thousand thieves are headed to Los Angeles," the *LA Times* warned in 1913. "The eastern departments recently sent word that nearly every thief caught said he would leave for Los Angeles if released, and further, that every man that was wanted was reported to be in Los Angeles or headed for the city."[4] Angelenos remembered how just a few years earlier, Al "Scarface" Capone had slipped into Los Angeles to enjoy the warm weather and the Hollywood scene before Chief James Davis ceremoniously escorted him out. What people did not know at the time was just how intricately LAPD was woven with organized crime and how deeply corruption had sunk within the Los Angeles mayor's, district attorney's, and city attorney's offices.

On August 31, 1933, Chief of Police James Edgar Davis held a summit with LA County Sheriff Eugene Biscailuz, District Attorney Buron Rogers Fitts, and various heads of gang and narcotics units, marshals, and judges. The purpose of this meeting of high-ranking officials was to form a "co-operative move to rid the city and its environs of hoodlums, bandits, and prowlers," said Fitts. Davis's calling of this top-level meeting was, in part, to battle a spate of killings among New York mobsters. But another main reason for the summit's urgency, wrote the *LA Times*, was the shooting of Allen and Withington.[5]

Calling crime-fighting forums such as this one was nothing new for Davis. In 1926, at age thirty-seven, he became the youngest-ever LAPD chief. This position was the last thing his family thought he could ever achieve. At age sixteen he had run away from home and then tried his hand as a cotton picker, cowpuncher, delivery man in a Wells Fargo office, soda bottler, field artilleryman in the US Army in the Philippines, street car conductor, and fireman. At age twenty-two, seeking more adventure but needing more consistent pay, Davis joined the Los Angeles Police Department as a patrolman. He quickly moved up the ranks, learning ordinances, effective police measures, and regulations. An avid hunter and fisherman, he considered moving north to become a member of the Canadian Northwest Mounted Police, but Davis fell in love with Edna Kline, married her in 1915, and built a bungalow in the Silver Lake neighborhood in which to start their large family. Davis's frugality extended to his family: When the home became crowded with five kids, he saw no reason to enlarge or reconfigure the house but rather just allowed the two older boys to dig themselves a room under the house in the back, where the hillside sloped down, and sleep there.[6]

Described by the press and his family as "hard-boiled" and "strictly business-like," the native Texan admitted to a biographer that he had an inferiority complex, as he had no father figure growing up and had not graduated from high school. He felt handicapped by these issues as he grew older, and sought a career that would help him overcome these psychological deficiencies. By the time he made detective lieutenant in the mid-1920s, he "suddenly woke up" and began to "study critically what was going on up ahead of me in the management of the police department." His biggest ambition was for Los Angeles to be "an unhealthy town for criminals of all kinds." He wished for crooks to steer clear of the City of Angels because they were too afraid to set foot in a town with a "relentless and uncompromising police force." Davis told an *LA Times* reporter that his police force must be relentless about running down and arresting crooks but also that the courts must cooperate by giving "sufficiently severe sentences." In 1926 Davis formed a fifty-man "gun squad," announcing that "the gun-toting element and the rum smugglers are going to learn that murder and gun-toting are most inimical.... I want them brought in dead, not alive and will reprimand any officer who shows the least mercy to a criminal."[7]

For the next three years, Chief Davis endeared himself to both the general public and the brass at the LAPD. The former appreciated his dry yet folksy humor, as well as his no-holds-barred approach to keeping crime at bay. The latter responded well to his red-baiting, ultra-right-of-center approach to police administration. Constitutional rights, Davis once remarked, were "of no benefit to anybody but crooks and criminals."[8] He made LAPD officers known worldwide as firearm experts. He initiated the dragnet system for tracking down wanted criminals, whereby the city was staked off into different sections in which officers stopped and examined all motorists and detained characters they deemed suspicious—similar to modern "stop and frisk" practices. The chief stressed the value of statistics for determining crime trends and fired more than 240 officers for "bad conduct."[9]

Still, for all the good that Davis had done for police officers in the city of Los Angeles, he was suddenly and summarily demoted to head of the traffic division in 1929 when John Clinton Porter, famously a xenophobe and a teetotaler, replaced George Edward Cryer as mayor of Los Angeles. Cryer, a capable administrator who had played a large part in securing Los Angeles as host for the 1932 Summer Olympic Games, could not deflect accusations of graft and mob ties, though none were ever proven. And although Cryer and Davis were often at odds with each other over departmental budgets, the reformers who called for Cryer's dismissal also called for Davis's. On October 31, 1929, the police commission charged Davis with incompetence and neglect of duty; he acquiesced to a demotion in order to save his pension.

Davis experienced a reversal of fortune on August 10, 1933. Republican Frank L. Shaw defeated Democratic incumbent Porter in the mayoral election and restored many favorites to the police commission. In turn, the commission put Davis back in his original vaunted position. And according to the *Times,* the *Herald-Express,* and other local papers, his leadership could not have come at a better time. The prospective repeal of the Eighteenth Amendment and possible end of Prohibition, the advent of racetrack gambling in California, the city's proximity to Mexico and to the sea, its high per-capita wealth, and its large population with thinly policed areas were just some of the reasons Southern California was luring more and more criminals from the East, according to the head of the police. "Chief Davis," wrote the *Times*, "knows the situation thoroughly and has already made plans to meet it. He plans to carry the fight to the enemy."[10]

"The enemy" for Chief Davis was not just the criminal element. The Los Angeles Police Department was facing a perception crisis. The first federal review of law enforcement in the United States—formed by President Herbert Hoover in 1929 and more commonly known as the Wickersham Report—was a largely flawed attempt to find better ways to enforce Prohibition laws and reduce alcohol-related crime. What the report did accomplish was to highlight many abuses of power by police and to show how politicized police management had become. *Calling All Cars* was a vehicle that would allow Davis to show that law enforcement was in control of a city that was seemingly run by criminals. Chief Davis himself introduced the real-life case in each week's episode, highlighting his knowledge of the case and, more importantly, suggesting his close supervision of his subordinates' activities and his commitment to solving crimes.[11] Material for the program, explained the *Times*, would be taken from the confidential police files of Davis, based on "facts," and in "no way objectionable or repulsive in presentation."[12] Sergeant Jesse Rosenquist, a real LAPD dispatcher, narrated portions of every episode throughout the entire series. The inaugural episode on November 29, 1933, dramatized the murder of a policeman a few months prior in a movie theater holdup in the tony Westwood section of West Los Angeles. But it was the Burmah White episode that received all the press.

Radio Guide magazine published a follow-up article about the *Cars* episode and had a few things to add about Burmah's traipse down the "Old Road to Sin":

"So convenient," she [Burmah] said it had been. Kisses led to midnight revels; and breathless, daring puffs at supposedly mild 'reefers' filled

with chopped stalks of the hashish-like marihuana [sic] weed finally led to injections of that most soul-shattering of all drugs, morphine. Tommy had the habit, and Burmah thought that it would be fun. She liked the thrills the drug gave her, the feeling that she could master the world, and the way everything appeared too screamingly funny for words after she had had a shot of the forbidden "snow."

But Tommy didn't have any money, explained *Radio Guide*, and neither did Burmah, so he took his "light o' love" on adventures to take money from "saps." "Only saps work," was Tom's credo, it said. Indeed, Tom beat Burmah, said the *Guide*, but "the thrill of the chase" and "the intensity of their love-making as the powerful opiate began to steal over them" were enough to make her forget about her bruises. Burmah was able to re-create this thrill over and over again by stealing from others too. A dozen witnesses, according to the *Guide*, identified her as the girl who had taken their money and watches while her companion held the gun—as the girl who had laughed with delight as Tommy White pulled the trigger.

Radio Guide wrote that Burmah had easily convinced Los Angeles's "sob sisters" (female columnists) that she was "an innocent dupe" in the hands of a "suave and handsome ex-convict." And yet, the article asked, why had she married Tom White of her own free will, before her parents and friends and before his sister? Why had she driven the stolen car in all his exploits and taken care of servicing it afterward so that he would never be seen? At any moment she could have left him, had she really wanted to. At the end of his investigation, the article concluded, the district attorney showed what Burmah Arline White really was: a "thrill-mad, dope-hungry little gun-moll with soft painted lips for her gunman lover and a hard heart and a shrill laugh for the victims he left weltering in their own blood."[13] These sentiments echoed an opinion piece run in the *Times* on November 7, 1933, the day after Burmah was sentenced:

Naturally the emotionalists writing for publicity disagree with the judge's declaration that young criminals must pay the penalty. Pampering and petting criminals and weeping over their having to pay the penalty is the stock in trade of the professional sob sister. Burmah's life has just begun, they wail, and how will it end if she's thrown into prison? That she had ample opportunity to leave and to denounce to the police the companion who was supposed to be terrorizing her—that she only became so terrorized after her defense counsel could find no other alibi for her—means nothing to sobsters. She has blue eyes and a pretty face—and so their hearts bleed for her.[14]

The *Times*'s and *Radio Guide*'s indictments of those who would feel sorry for Burmah were of course dramatized. Indeed, the date of publication for the *Times* opinion piece proves that the writer would have had a hard time gathering other reactions to Judge Fletcher Bowron's sentence, which he had just given the afternoon prior. The most sympathetic portrayals of the teen—such as those found in her hometown newspaper, the *Santa Ana Times*—stopped short of analyzing the psychology behind her exploits with Tom White and merely described what she was like growing up. But there were two "sob sisters" who held considerable sway in the court of public opinion and who offered a much more nuanced view of Burmah White as a human being. These columnists were Louella Oettinger Parsons and Agness "Aggie" May Underwood.

In 1922 Louella Parsons began writing movie news for newspaper giant William Randolph Hearst. He was so pleased with the popularity of the Illinois native's work that he gave her a syndicated column at the then-unheard-of salary of $250 a week. She won her own fame by writing about the people of Hollywood, and at the height of her popularity, in the fall of 1933, Parsons was syndicated in 407 daily and Sunday papers as the $52,000-a-year motion picture editor of the International News Service. Flush from her "success" at breaking the news of Mary Pickford and Douglas Fairbanks's marital split in March of that year and an exclusive with elusive playwright George Bernard Shaw in July, Parsons approached Burmah in jail and took down her story:

"Girl Bandit Says 'Snake' Terrified Her into Crime"

Los Angeles, September 23, 1933

The 19-year-old blonde bandit, Burmah Adams White, arrested at a time when the whole town is screaming vengeance against gangsters and their trail of crime, has found herself without one sympathetic friend.

The picture of a girl who drove a car for a hardened criminal so that he might shoot down unsuspecting victims and rob them is not a pretty one. Decent people shudder at the crimes in which she is involved.

But did Burmah get enjoyment out of watching her bridegroom plunder his unfortunate victims? She says no.

Experienced newspaper reporters who interviewed her assured me that here was a phenomenon, a girl born without knowing the difference between right and wrong.

I am sorry to disagree! Burmah Adams White is not a moral degenerate. She is only a young girl who has been unfortunate enough to get into bad company and to fall in love with a man who had lived a full life of crime before his evil eyes were attracted by her slim, blonde beauty.

I am not trying to condone a crime as shocking as the shooting down of the school teacher and her escort. I have only horror for the part Burmah played when she drove the car and sat and watched Thomas White blind an innocent woman with an uncalled for shot from his gangster gun.

But Burmah says that she was under the cruel domination of Thomas White. This she told me herself after I had won her confidence. She was in deadly terror of him and was as stunned as her own parents when she learned the supposed prosperous business man she had married was a cheap crook who preyed on society and made his living by theft and murder.

Burmah's confidence didn't come easily. I had gone to the Hall of Justice to interview her on a story that she had saved the life of Ricardo Cortez after Thomas White had jealously tried to shoot him down because his young wife had written to ask for Cortez's picture.[15]

The look of defiance she wore when the matron introduced me changed to one of withering scorn.

"I wouldn't even know Mr. Cortez if I saw him," she said. "My screen favorites are George Arliss and Lionel Barrymore. The fantastic

Cortez yarn is on par with some of the lies that have been told about me.

"My mother," she said in a whisper, "came to see me today. She said that I am more normal than she has seen me in months. I am not a bad girl. I . . ." then she stopped.

"Go on," I urged, "please tell me."

"Oh, what's the use? The thing is done and my life is over."

"What were you going to tell me?" I persisted.

"I want you to know that it isn't true that I picked Thomas White up in the streets. I met him at a dance. I was introduced to him; and he was kind and thoughtful and polite. It was only after I married him that I knew I was in the clutches of a fiend.

"I was so terrified that I did exactly as he told me to do. That's why I am here in jail."

What's the end? Only tears and heartache. A pity that Thomas White hadn't met his death before he dragged this 19-year-old girl down to this hopeless abyss.[16]

No doubt Louella Parsons was one of the "emotionalists" the *Times* referred to as heaping too much pity on Burmah.

Agness "Aggie" Underwood was no less ambitious than Parsons. Though both women covered goings-on in Hollywood and Los Angeles in general, Underwood focused less on gossip and film stories than Parsons did and more on the "underbelly" of the city—she liked to solve mysteries as opposed to being the first to announce an engagement or divorce. Her sources were film stars too, but also prostitutes, bartenders, gangsters, and government officials. Historian Joan Renner describes Underwood as a young wife and mother who, in 1926, desperately wanted some extra money for new stockings and the occasional pair of shoes, so she took a temporary position as a switchboard operator for the *Los Angeles Record*. In December 1927 the city was horrified by the kidnapping and cruel mutilation murder of twelve-year-old schoolgirl Marion Parker. Aggie was at the *Record* when they received word that the perpetrator, William Edward Hickman, who had nicknamed himself "The Fox," had been captured in Oregon. The breaking story created a firestorm of activity in the newsroom—Aggie had never seen anything like it. She knew then that she didn't want to be a bystander. It didn't take long, according to Renner, for Aggie to realize that she loved the newspaper business and wanted to become a reporter.

Like Parsons, Hearst hired Underwood too, snapping her up for his Los Angeles *Evening Herald and Express* when the *Record* was sold in January 1935. Hearst was impressed by Underwood's ability to gain the confidence of Nellie May Madison, the first woman to be sentenced to death in the state of California (her sentence was later commuted to life in prison).[17] In May and June of 1934, before Madison's trial, Underwood had been the only reporter to speak at length with her; the imprisoned woman was the first female criminal Underwood had examined closely, and she was fascinated, so much so that she decided that women and crime would be her "beat." Underwood wasted no time planning a series of features about Madison and her fellow inmates at the California Institution for Women at Tehachapi. Clara Phillips, imprisoned for murdering her husband's alleged paramour with a club hammer in 1926, was the first in the series; Burmah was the last.

"Burmah White Pays Debt for Wrongs in Bitterness" was, as its headline suggests, a feature that portrayed the blonde as thoughtful and repentant . . . but also perhaps bitter about being punished. When she was first brought to Tehachapi in the spring of 1934, she was "full of ambition," according to Underwood, and taught English, typing, and drama to fellow inmates—she had taken theater in high school. But then, according to the essay, Burmah fell ill for almost two months, and with that illness came the realization of the severity of her penalty, that parole was not possible, and that the best years of her life must be spent paying her debt to society.[18]

"I've gone into it very thoroughly," she told Underwood, her first visitor since November 1934. "The prison board can't do a thing. The judge who sentenced me fixed that up and I just can't see any sense in working hard every day when there's nothing to work for. I can't see any sense hoping for the future when there's nothing to hope for. I can't see any sense in training for work to do when I get out of here, because I'll be an old lady then—maybe not old physically, but I know from what it's already done to me that I'll be hundreds of years old mentally." In the caption underneath a photo of Burmah clasping her hands together, Underwood noted that the prisoner's "tough demeanor" was gone and she lived "aloof," thinking of her crime—though it also says she thought about her long sentence.[19]

The radio programs, Parsons, and Underwood probably used James "Jimmy" Shambra's interview with Burmah shortly after her arrest as a foundation for their questions to the "blonde moll." Shambra was another *Herald and Express* reporter—one who was just starting his career at the paper at the time of Burmah's arrest. At age twenty-five, Shambra was already an established police beat writer and often sat in arrestee interviews alongside the LAPD. The cub scribe cut his teeth on the crime beat with his 1931 interview of Winnie Ruth Judd, who was sentenced to death for her role in murdering two friends and transporting their dismembered bodies from Phoenix to Los Angeles by train, causing the press to dub the crimes the "trunk murders." He interviewed Burmah within days of her arrest and attempted to give readers insight as to why a "good girl" would go bad:

> *How did Burmah Adams White get that way? What is the psychological background of a girl of 19, who callously watched her sweetheart shoot and blind a woman teacher and a few days later married the gunman, get that way? Burmah White has a lot of self-pity and apparently no pity for others. Herewith she tells her version of her life story up to the time she started out as the blonde moll of "Rattlesnake" White. The rest of her story with its drab background of robbery and gunfire was confessed today to District Attorney Fitts.[20]*

Shambra's version of Burmah's life story and reasons for going into a life of crime was almost certainly embellished or even made up out of whole cloth in parts to better frame an inherent personality for a young woman who would commit crime and think she could get away with it. White allegedly recounted how she remembered learning her ABCs faster than anybody in her kindergarten class and how she rebelliously refused to come inside from the sandbox when the bell rang. But other portions can be corroborated by other sources, such as interviews with her parents and later schoolteachers that suggest she was a very bright pupil and liked to study. After all, she did skip a grade, and she earned top marks every year of her education. Thus, Shambra's explanation of how she "got off track" was probably some version of Burmah's own tale but—like with all the other interviews with her—was shaped by the artistic nature of the interviewer. Some portions were bolded for effect:

First I was a pupil in the Julius E. [sic] Lathrop junior high school, where, just a dumb kid as far as knowing anything besides school and studies were concerned, I was duly graduated after I'd finished the ninth grade[.] Then I became a full-fledged high school girl, enrolling in the Santa Ana High School.

I went there for two years, with my life all work and no play, with my daily schedule about as interesting and exciting as a congressional report. I would get up at a certain time, wash my face, brush my teeth, eat breakfast and go to school. Then in the afternoon I would study after school and at night go to bed early.

I wasn't allowed to have any boy friends, but I didn't know what I was missing at that time. *When I was ready to enter my senior year, however, I decided I wasn't learning much in high school and so I quit and went to a beauty culture school. I intended to be the best cosmotolist [sic] there ever was. I have always believed every girl should equip herself to earn a living, anyway.*

About this time my father and mother weakened a little and let me go with boys. I could step out two nights a week, but I had to be home by 11 o'clock. Lots of times I just squeezed in as the clock was striking the hour, like Cinderella, and at other times I must admit I was a little later—but not by much.

Then I was graduated, got my diploma and everything, and there I was, a young and not bad-looking girl equipped to earn her own living and only Santa Ana to do it in. The prospect didn't look so good. Santa Ana is only a little burg after all. So I went to Balboa beach while the summer season was at its height and after working a week in a beauty shop opened one of my own. I had just exactly $1 capital, but my assurance was worth $1,000,000. I got by, too;

arranged for equipment on credit and ran that shop for about eight months.[21]

It was during those days that my first big romance put in appearance. The man in the case was a business man—without much business as it turned out, later—but I thought he was swell.

I loved him, in fact, as much as any 17-year-old girl could love anybody. He was good-looking and romantic and girls fall for that kind, you know.

We went to shows and dances and had a wonderful time. Not public dances—I think they're cheap and common. I never could get used to having a stranger slap you on the back and say: "Hi, baby! How's for the next dance?" I was a demure little thing in those days, anyway. I hadn't even blonded my hair, though I certainly knew how to do it, all right.

Burmah's then-boyfriend, she said, left without telling her and broke her heart. She attributed this to the fact that he was broke and discouraged. She was sad at first, but as time went on, her heart healed and she decided a change of scenery would help her forget about it entirely. She and friend "Betty," though they only had about ten dollars between them, decided to move to the "big city": Los Angeles. In early 1933 they did just that, and both got jobs at beauty parlors.

Incidentally, I blonded by my hair the day before we went on this excursion. It has always seemed to me [that] blondes get by better than brunettes.[22]

True Story magazine purportedly let Burmah tell the story of her life and the events of the weeks leading up to Tom's shooting and her arrest. The publication also sponsored a radio program that dramatized select stories that it printed. *True Story's The Court of Human Relations* featured actual court cases that were re-created by actors; listeners then were asked to write in with the verdicts they would have chosen if they were jurors and explain why. Michele Hilmes, in *Only Connect: A Cultural History of Broadcasting in the United States*, described the program as "a forerunner of much of the material on Court TV or *Judge Judy*." In a typical story, a young woman tells of being seduced then abandoned by some fellow who proves unworthy. She, after bearing a child out of wedlock, for example, tries hard to put her life back together again. The end was always moral, but *The Court of Human Relations* owed its success to making sure that its listeners—just like the readers of *True Story*—fully savored the "adventure of a sinful liaison."[23] The program began airing in January 1934; the "Burmah White" episode aired Sunday, April 15, 1934.

"Probably nothing since Theodore Dreiser's 'American Tragedy,'" said a syndicated newspaper article days before the airing, "has had so much to cause sober reflection upon society's share in the crime problem as the true story of Burmah White, 19-year-old Santa Ana (California) girl sentenced to from 30 years to life in prison."[24]

There is no surviving script or audio for Burmah's eponymous install-ment, but *Radio Mirror* wrote about it:

> One story that aroused a great deal of attention was the case of Bur-mah White. Although it is the policy of the magazine to change the real names of the characters in the stories it prints, an exception was made in the case of Burmah White, 19-year-old California girl, sentenced to serve a prison term of from thirty years to life as the accomplice of her husband, shot dead resisting arrest.
>
> The White story was full of pathos. The child of respectable parents, Burmah had chosen to become self-supporting in her teens and secured employment in a beauty parlor where she met another girl who intro-duced her to Tom White, ex-convict, who was to spread terror in Los Angeles as the dread "rattlesnake bandit."

Too late, the piece said, Burmah learned of her beau's real identity and was forced to accompany him, driving stolen automobiles on his forays. Tom, it said, had only married her to protect himself from the law—a reader or listener might have gotten the impression that it might have been more pitiful for Burmah that Tom married her without love than it was that he married her to prevent her from testifying against him.

Whatever the case, *The Court of Human Relations* reflected in its broadcast, public opinion against Burmah was in "white heat." Overtly complicit or under duress, the moll did not realize until the end of her real trial that "she was being called upon to answer for the sins of her bridegroom in full measure." The cast of this episode charged every moment of the story with "dramatic intensity." And then the letters started pouring in to the Contest Department of McFadden Communications, the publisher of *True Story*:

> *Three out of every five of the letters received declared Burmah White was not guilty in their eyes and three out of five asked that she be given a new trial. Another fifth of the verdicts felt that she was guilty but the sentence was excessive. There were a scattering of opinions among the remaining fifth, ranging all the way from three who found her guilty as charged and deserving of the sentence, to those who would place the entire blame upon society, which permitted Tom White, a dangerous criminal, to be at liberty.*[25]

On November 6, 1933, Orange County's KREG featured psychologist H. L. Parks on its "Health and Happiness" segment. Parks spoke of the Burmah White case and offered opinions as to its psychological aspects, opinions of various people involved in the case, and a discussion of its "relationship to young people today." And in 1940, when the *Los Angeles Evening Herald and Express* decided to mine some of its more sensational stories for radio show episodes, the "Burmah White Story" became one of its first, airing July 28, 1940, on Southern California's KFI radio station.[26]

At the end of the Burmah White episode of *Calling All Cars*, Chief Davis cautioned the citizens of Los Angeles and the country at large: "This series of crimes in which Burmah White participated . . . [she] would never have entered a career of crime had the parole system been stringent enough to prevent desperadoes from having their freedom. It is my sincere hope that you, the citizens, will demand a proper parole system so that you and yours will not be in constant danger from the ruthless viciousness of men of the stripe of Tom White."[27]

49

CHAPTER 5

Trial, Part I

GEORGE STAHLMAN LIKED TO BE CALLED "THE HANGMAN" BY FRIENDS and family. He sent twelve people to the noose during his tenure as chief prosecutor for the City of Los Angeles in the 1930s.[1] Born in Kansas in 1900 to German immigrants, Stahlman joined the US Navy at sixteen and served in World War I as a mail ship operator and electrician. He married a young woman from his hometown before the war was officially over, but they divorced a few years later. He moved west, attended Southern California Law School (later renamed University of Southern California), and was admitted to the bar in 1925. Two years later, Stahlman joined the office of Buron Fitts and began litigating in earnest. He fell in love with Los Angeles and with movie actress Viola Evans, whom he married in 1930 on the Metro-Goldwyn-Mayer studio lot.

Stahlman became a regular feature in newspapers soon after he began work as deputy district attorney. In November 1929 the young attorney filed adultery charges against George N. Sunday, son of famous evangelist Billy Sunday, and a woman named Myrna La Salle, a twenty-four-year-old model and divorcée. The younger Sunday was married; one night, his wife and an LAPD detective burst in and found him and LaSalle in bed together at midnight. Dismissing LaSalle's claims that they were "just reading together," Stahlman arrested both. Just a year after Burmah's trial, Stahlman was one of the prosecutors who successfully convicted Nellie Madison of murder; as noted earlier, she was the first woman to be sentenced to death in the state of California.[2]

The other prosecutor assigned to the people's case against Burmah was Grant Cooper, just a few years younger than Stahlman at thirty years

old, spry, and clean-cut even by the standards of the day. He was a gradu-
ate of Los Angeles's Southwestern College of Law. Mr. Cooper never
intended to become a lawyer. He dropped out of high school back in New
York and had several odd jobs before coming to California as a hired hand
on an oil tanker. An uncle persuaded him to go into a more genteel profession and join him at his law firm if he could pass the bar exam, which
he did in 1927.

Shortly after receiving his license to practice, Cooper appeared in
headlines as counsel for Bert Wallis, an LAPD captain of detectives who,
along with other high-ranking officers and two newspaper reporters,
charged into a home at 4372 Beagle Street on the evening of August
5, 1927, allegedly responding to an anonymous call of a "wild party" in
progress. He and his colleagues arrested City Councilman Carl Ingold
Jacobson, who was supposedly stripped down to his underwear and about
to have relations with the owner of the house, a constituent. Jacobson,
a vocal "vice-crusader," was arrested on morals charges. The councilman
asked to be taken to jail, but instead Wallis first took him to the home of
Police Commissioner Rodney Webster. A couple of years later, Jacobson
told a magazine reporter that Webster said, "It doesn't pay to write letters to the police commission and get them published, does it?" Captain
Wallis then took Jacobson to the Chamber of Commerce Building downtown, where the police intelligence unit kept a secret satellite office. Loyal
Durand "L. D." Hotchkiss, then city editor of the *L.A. Times*, and District
Attorney Asa Keyes were waiting there. Keyes later testified that although
this was city business, he was called in to "advise," as the city prosecutor
could not be located. If Jacobson would just sign the blank confession he
gave him, Keyes purportedly said, they could "forget" the whole thing.
Jacobson refused, and he went to trial on September 14, 1927.

The jury in Jacobson's trial deadlocked, and the morals charges levied
against him were dropped. But two years later, Jacobson sued Wallis and
four other detectives along with three gangsters, accusing them of conspiracy. This time the female "victim" from Beagle Street switched sides and
testified for Jacobson. Cooper defended Ellis again, ferociously attacking
Jacobson's character, shouting comparisons between the councilman and
Benedict Arnold and Judas Iscariot. The jury deliberated for seventy-nine

hours before announcing they could not reach a verdict, and the ordeal resulted in a mistrial. A new trial in June 1929 also ended in a mistrial.

During his subsequent years as a prosecutor, Cooper won many death penalty convictions. Later in his career, the prosecutor switched to defense attorney and became a vocal opponent of the death penalty, arguing that it did not work as a deterrent. Cooper later became well known around the country as the energetic defense attorney of Sirhan Sirhan, who assassinated US Senator Robert Kennedy, and for his representation of other notables, including mob boss Johnny Roselli and actress Shirley Temple in her divorce from her first husband.

Friday, October 20, 1933, at 9:50 a.m., a policewoman brought Burmah Arline Adams White into the Los Angeles Superior Court room of Honorable Judge Fletcher Bowron. The jurist was not as famous then as he would one day become as mayor of Los Angeles, but his star was ascending quickly.

Bowron was born in Poway, California, on August 13, 1887, to parents who had migrated from the Midwest and formed a citrus and dairy corporation. He was the youngest of three children and graduated from Los Angeles High School in 1904. He attended the University of California, Berkeley, from 1907 to 1909, and then began studies at USC Law School but dropped out to work as a newspaper reporter in Oakland, San Francisco, and Los Angeles. A few years later he returned to law school and was admitted to the California bar in 1917. Shortly thereafter, when the United States entered World War I, Bowron enlisted in the US Army, where he served in the 14th Field Artillery for a few months before transferring to the Military Intelligence Division. He was based in Los Angeles.

It is not clear what Bowron's official duties were at the Military Intelligence Division, but not two weeks after his transfer to this division on February 1, 1918, newspapers covered his explosive testimony to a federal commissioner about a conversation he overheard between two men planning to ship arms to Pancho Villa's army in Mexico. Two months later, Bowron charged a man and woman with racketeering, arguing that the woman's intercepted letters used code words to defraud a patriotic fundraising organization.[3]

After the war's end, Bowron worked divorce cases before going into a more general practice with Z. Bertrand West, son of a Los Angeles Superior Court judge, but he quickly moved on to a more visible position. In late 1922 Bowron's friend in the Los Angeles courthouse pressroom, Edwin M. Daugherty, was appointed state corporation commissioner and convinced Bowron to join his staff as a deputy in the Los Angeles office. In this position, the young attorney aggressively sued the powerful Julian Petroleum Corporation for investor fraud, and caught the attention of Governor Friend Richardson, a Republican. Richardson hired Bowron to be his executive secretary, a post he had held for only about six months when the governor appointed him to fill a Superior Court vacancy. On October 5, 1926, the thirty-nine-year-old took the bench in the Superior Court of Los Angeles, in the big Victorian-style red sandstone building at Temple and Broadway.[4]

Minutes after policewoman Lula Lane un-handcuffed Burmah, Bowron stalked into his domain with his requisite black robe flowing behind him and asked everyone to be seated. He allowed prosecutor Cooper to call roll with the people's witnesses. When he finished, defense attorney George Francis asked for a continuance of the case because Donald MacKay had been hospitalized for pleurisy. MacKay's doctor testified to the seriousness of the attorney's condition but thought he would be able to return to court in five days. Stahlman balked. "Your Honor realizes," he said, "there are 28 witnesses here in court. Mr. Crombie Allen came to my office, yesterday, and informed me that he has to be available to leave the country on a trip; he has made arrangements for some time past. . . . He is an essential and necessary witness." Moreover, Stahlman argued, "I don't know how many other witnesses, of course, might be inconvenienced by a long continuance." Cooper asked if Francis could stand in for MacKay, but Francis protested that he had not been asked to be a part of Burmah's permanent defense team and was merely filling in for MacKay temporarily. Also, Francis continued, he was a civil attorney and was scheduled to start work on a different trial the following week.[5]

Stahlman pressed forcefully for the trial to begin immediately. Besides the fact that his witnesses would be inconvenienced should it be delayed, he argued, Bowron's calendar would be terribly disrupted. The attorney knew this would strike the right chord with Bowron: The jurist was a vocal proponent of reforming Los Angeles's congested court calendars and a few years later he would be the first judge to institute a pretrial division in Superior Court, in which prosecutors and defendants were required to meet at least ten days before proceedings and decide the number of witnesses and other matters, and perhaps speed up out-of-court settlements.

Despite George Francis's best efforts, Bowron decided that the trial should start immediately. "Have you any attorney other than Donald MacKay employed at this time?" he asked Burmah. She said no.

A few days later, on October 26, Burmah sat in court without counsel. The *Examiner* took a photo of her with her head slightly tucked into her black fur-collared jacket. The caption that ran with the photo in that evening's edition read, "These candid camera photos snapped in court today show the emotions of 'icy blonde' Burmah White, widow of the slain 'rattlesnake' bandit, when she went on trial charged with participating in a series of holdups and brutal shootings. With cold eyes she watched the selection of the jury."[6] MacKay was still sick. His brother, Olin, appeared in front of the bench to ask for a brief continuance, pleading ignorance of the facts of the case and his inexperience with criminal law in general:

> *BOWRON: Are you not associated with your brother in the practice of law?*

> *OLIN N. MACKAY: I am associated with him, your Honor. I try mostly civil cases, however.*

> *JUDGE BOWRON: Are you not familiar with the defense in this case?*

> *OLIN N. MACKAY: I know nothing about the circumstances of the case other than what I have read in the paper, your Honor.*

> *JUDGE BOWRON: Well, I advised the defendant to be ready for trial today, and also advised that if her counsel continued to be ill, by*

reason of the large number of witnesses and the number of pending cases, and the condition of the calendar, that it would be necessary to proceed.

OLIN N. MACKAY: I would ask time, if your Honor please. I realize that I have not at the present moment given all that might be required for a legal sowing for a continuance. It will be necessary for me to go to the Glendale Research Hospital with a stenographer, in order to get a statement from the doctor as to his [brother Donald's] condition today; but I feel that in justice to the defendant she should have the opportunity to have the counsel that she has selected and who has prepared the case for trial, and is ready to go to trial the minute that he is physically able to. There is absolutely no reason as far as the defendant is concerned why this case should not go to trial at the present moment . . . but this is a very important case for the defendant, as well as for the People; and I believe that she is entitled to be properly represented in this matter.[7]

Bowron denied this request. He appointed Olin and George Francis as Burmah's defense attorneys. While a messenger sent for Francis, who was working at his other trial, the judge instructed the clerk to fill the jury box. Francis appeared an hour or so later, most likely out of breath, reiterating the fact that he was involved in a hearing at the Supreme Court in which the City of Los Angeles was a party. Francis begged Judge Bowron to consider his position and to find someone else to represent Burmah, even if she were amenable to having him do so. He told Bowron that he was perfectly willing to do so but that he was "not at all prepared or at all qualified, in fact, to undertake to give this defendant anywhere near the representation that my meager knowledge of the case leads me to believe that she is entitled to." And most importantly, the attorney importuned, he had never tried a criminal case in the state of California, and despite Burmah's confidence in him, he would be "somewhat of a detriment to her."[8] Again, Bowron denied this request and added Francis to Burmah's defense.

George Haywood Francis was a very skilled attorney. The son of a prominent educator in Pasadena, he attended law school in his father's native Ohio, and even clerked for Clarence Darrow in 1924, working on his "thrill killers" case concerning the murder of a teenaged boy. Francis married for the first time when he was just a teen; that union quickly failed. He wed his second wife, Sally, before finishing law school. The pair moved to Los Angeles in 1925, and Francis immediately got a job within the Los Angeles City Prosecutor's office, which later merged with the City Attorney's office.

But Francis was a loner and grew uncomfortable with the politics and spotlight of the downtown office where he was frequently called upon to defend people accused of high-profile murders or fraud. He asked to be transferred to the Harbor Division. There he dealt with port leases and inventory papers as opposed to people. The politics followed him there, though: His boss Erwin C. Werner and the mayor demanded that Francis serve several oil companies with law suits, charging that these companies had not paid on canceled charters. It soon became obvious to Francis that Werner wanted him to uncover misdeeds or mistakes made by the harbor commissioner, an appointee of the previous mayor. When he would not, Werner suspended him without pay—until so many public employees gave newspaper interviews in support of Francis that Mayor Porter forced Werner to reinstate him.[9]

The third of the trio of attorneys representing Burmah was Robert "Bob" Wheeler. The mild-mannered and unassuming only child of a wholesale bottler, Wheeler had not planned to be a lawyer. But he grew to love the law while employed as a bailiff in the Los Angeles Supreme Court. He entered Southwestern College of Law in 1927, where he also became assistant debate coach. A native of Los Angeles, Wheeler was admitted to the bar in 1931.

Court was adjourned for the day.[10]

The next day, Burmah's parents and little sister, Jo, sat next to her in the front-row bench of the courtroom while Stahlman made his opening statement and read the charges against her: seven counts of robbery, one count of attempted robbery, and three counts of assault with a deadly weapon.[11] Leslie Bartel was the first witness called to the stand. Defense attorney Francis interjected: "At this time, your Honor, please, I should like also to make a motion excluding all of the witnesses from the court room." Cooper countered: "Your Honor, the only thought I have to suggest is this: that with the great number of witnesses we haven't any convenient place for them to stay." Bowron concurred. All witnesses would stay.

In all US states today, either side in a criminal trial can ask the judge to exclude witnesses from the courtroom while another witness testifies. This is usually done before the trial begins by filing a motion for sequestration. Essentially, each witness testifies without being influenced by other testimony. This reduces any chance of witnesses tailoring their testimony to match or clash someone else's. Sequestered witnesses do not go into the courtroom until it is their turn to testify.[12] But at the time of Burmah's trial, allowing witnesses in the courtroom during testimony was the prerogative of the presiding judge.

For the most part, there was no argument from either the defense or prosecution side about what actually transpired the day of September 6, 1933, when Tom was shot dead by police and Burmah was arrested, nor was there much dispute about the events that took place during the three weeks or so leading up to that fateful day. But some of the witnesses' accounts of their experience with Tom and Burmah White were terrifying.

Burmah acted as the getaway driver for many of Tom White's armed robberies and shootings until September 5, when the pair "cooled off" and mostly stayed inside their apartment building while Pearl and Jo Adams stayed with Burmah to attend some of Jo's nearby doctor's appointments. What was in dispute throughout the trial, however, was Burmah's demeanor during these crimes and, more specifically, whether she seemed coerced or not or had the opportunity to get away from Tom at any time.

George Cooper made robbery victim Clarence Campfield Lewis recount his encounter with Tom White on August 31, 1933, in meticulous detail. This was important because it was the first time Tom (and therefore Burmah) could be definitively tied to an attempt to fire a gun at somebody besides Crombie Allen and Cora Withington. After White fired a first shot and missed, Lewis punched him in the face.

The prosecution called a couple more witnesses: a grocery clerk at a Safeway store and a newspaper boy. Neither could say whether Burmah was driving the getaway car or whether there had actually been a

woman in the vehicle at all. Nonetheless, Cooper and Stahlman successfully established Tom and Burmah's methodology: Tom would approach
an individual or business, while Burmah revved the engine of a stolen car
and whisked him away when he finished. It would be difficult for any
reasonable person to believe that anyone *but* Burmah and Tom had committed any robberies involving a car within the month of August and the
first week of September 1933.

For the next day and a half of the trial, LAPD officers Arthur "A. J."
Bergeron, William Chester Burris, and Berthel Glen "B. G." Anderson
testified to what happened the day of September 6, 1933. Harry Richard
Maxwell, the fourth officer who was part of the initial foray into the Whites'
apartment that day, did not appear in court, and no explanation was given.

The statements from the three officers were virtually identical. The
men, dressed as auto mechanics, observed a woman they assumed was
Burmah White at a service station at Third and Carondelet Streets. They
followed her stolen maroon vehicle to the rear entrance of the Casa Del
Monte apartment house at 236 South Coronado. They met with a manager on the bottom floor and got directions to Apartment 18, where
Burmah resided with her mother and sister. Detective Burris's account is
perhaps the most detailed about what happened next:

*STAHLMAN: Now, you went into the apartment house through the
front door, I presume?*

*BURRIS: No. We went into the rear door of the apartment house.
Officers Anderson and Maxwell stayed at the back door while Bergeron
and myself went down and talked to the landlord.*

*STAHLMAN: And then you had some conversation with the land-
lord. And after that, where did you go?*

BURRIS: We went to Apartment 18.

*STAHLMAN: Now, when you arrived at Apartment 18 the four of
you were together. Is that right?*

BURRIS: Together, yes.

STAHLMAN: Who entered the apartment first?

BURRIS: Well, I don't recall. I remember Maxwell and Anderson and I were all together as we started into the door. In fact, we were all in one bunch, and, as I stepped in the door, I noticed the defendant, sitting over on a davenport with a lady that I later learned was her mother. And, as I entered the door, I said, "That is her," and stepped over to the davenport and took hold of her arm and told her to stand up. Just about the time she got on to her feet, I looked around, and I did not see Anderson or Bergeron, but Maxwell was looking into the kitchen. I heard a shot, and Maxwell ran from the apartment. And I just stayed there and held on to her arm.

STAHLMAN: Now, then, did you hear two other shots, Officer?

BURRIS: Well, I don't know how many shots.

STAHLMAN: You heard some shooting out in the hall?

BURRIS: I heard some shots.

STAHLMAN: Now, had you any conversation with her, other than telling her to stand up, previous to the time you heard the shooting?

BURRIS: No; I had not had time to talk to her.

STAHLMAN: Now, after the shooting—I will withdraw that question for the moment. You say you saw another woman there, who you later learned was her mother?

BURRIS: Yes.

STAHLMAN: No other persons in the apartment?

BURRIS: And a little girl, who she told me was her little sister.

STAHLMAN: About how old was that little girl?

BURRIS: I should judge approximately seven or eight years old.

STAHLMAN: Now, did you have some conversation with her then, after the shooting was over?

BURRIS: Yes.

STAHLMAN: Who was present at that conversation?

BURRIS: Well, I believe when I asked her the first question only her mother and little sister and the defendant and myself were in the room.

STAHLMAN: Did someone else come in after the conversation started?

BURRIS: Yes.

STAHLMAN: Who was that?

BURRIS: Maxwell, and I believe Bergeron came in after a few minutes.

STAHLMAN: Now, at that conversation, that occurred at Apartment 18 on that day, were any threats or force or violence used upon this defendant?

BURRIS: There was not.

STAHLMAN: Any offer of immunity or hope of reward extended to her?

BURRIS: There was not.

STAHLMAN: Were the statements that she made on that occasion free and voluntary?

STAHLMAN: Yes, sir.

Burris related what happened next. He asked the young woman he encountered in Apartment 18 what her name was. "Burmah Adams," she said. And then he peppered her with more questions:

BURRIS: What is your boy friend's name?

BURMAH: Tom White.

BURRIS: Where does he live?

BURMAH: Up on the next floor.

BURRIS: How long have you known him?

BURMAH: About two months.

BURRIS: Where did you meet him?

BURMAH: At a party.

BURRIS: Where is his gun?

BURMAH: What gun?

BURRIS: The .32–20.

BURMAH: I don't know anything about a gun.

BURRIS: I am interested in a .32–20 that you used the night you shot the man and woman out at 3rd and Occidental.

Burmah now began to whisper to him, according to Burris. "Don't tell my mother anything about this," she pleaded. Officer Burris recalled that he assured her he would not and then asked again, "Where is his gun, if you know?" "If he hasn't got it on him," she replied, "it is up in his room." Burris thought he might have bought Burmah's cooperation at this point but then found himself frustrated by her anxieties and her real or perceived obstinance:

BURRIS: Where is your car?

BURMAH: I haven't any car.

BURRIS: Where is the Chevrolet?

BURMAH: I haven't any Chevrolet.

BURRIS: Yes, you have, because I saw you just driving out of the filling station, just a few minutes ago, down here on Third Street.[13]

According to Burris, Burmah again begged him not to tell her mother. He assured her that he would not but asked her whether she thought that might be a moot point, since Mrs. Adams was bound to read about it in the newspapers sooner or later. "Well, let her find out about it later," Burmah replied. Burris picked up his interrogation again. Burmah finally admitted that she had the keys in her purse and opened that up. "Are those the keys that belong to the Chevrolet?" Burris asked. "Yes," she replied. "Are those the keys that you took off the man the night you took his car away from him?" "Yes," she said. Burris saw an opening, and he took it:

BURRIS: How many jobs have you been on?

BURMAH: Oh, not so many.

BURRIS: Well, you were with him over on the Third and Occidental case, where the woman was shot, weren't you?

BURMAH: (Whispering) Yes.

BURRIS: You were on the job out on Western, where he took a couple of shots at a man, weren't you?

BURMAH: Yes.

BURRIS: Wasn't you on one or two Safeway store jobs?

BURMAH: Well, can't I tell you about that later?

BURRIS: Well, it is alright. The only thing is, I would like to get the thing straight.

Burris told the court that his interrogation of Burmah was interrupted by one of his LAPD colleagues, who walked into her apartment and said, "Well, he was shot. He opened up on us and we shot him." According to Burris, a doctor on the scene pronounced Tom dead, and almost simultaneously a reporter came in to where the detective was standing with Burmah and started asking questions. "Maybe you would rather give him your name?" Burris asked Burmah. "Well," she said to the reporter, "my name is Burmah White from now on."[14]

Besides some minor differences in recollection of exact wording and where everyone stood, the police recounted that Thomas White walked down the landing from his fourth floor, toward the bunch. "We are policemen," Anderson said, and when they got a few feet away from him, Tom suddenly whirled and fired once. "At that time," the officer continued, "we both fired; and he started to fall backwards over the banister; and as he did, he fired another shot, and at that time I fired another one, myself."

Anderson fired two shots; Bergeron fired one. None of the officers were hit; White was hit three times.

It was the testimony of the officers that allowed both the prosecution and defense attorneys to try to frame Burmah's state of mind and whether she appeared to be under duress or abused during any or all of her relationship with White, up to and including his death. Francis took the first opportunity to open this door when he cross-examined Bergeron:

FRANCIS: Now, at the time [of her arrest] did you see any bruises on her face?

BERGERON: I noticed a bruise on her face when we got to Central Station, a black and blue mark, I should judge, if I remember rightly, around her head or neck—no, it was on her forehead, I remember now.

FRANCIS: From the time that you first observed the defendant, Burmah White, that afternoon, until the time upon which you noticed the bruise on her face that you have just mentioned, she had no scuffle with you or with any of the officers in which she could have gotten that bruise?

BERGERON: None that I know of. I had not been in the apartment until I had gone in there to call for the ambulance.

FRANCIS: Well, was not the bruise on her face the first time you noticed her?

BERGERON: I did not pay any attention to it. It might have been there.

FRANCIS: Did Burmah White tell you at any time after the shooting that you have described that you were lucky that Tom White had not shot you and herself, as well—that he had told her that he would shoot any officer who came to arrest him?

Bowron sustained a hearsay objection by Cooper. Stahlman called witness B. G. Anderson, a policeman, who described how the officers found and cornered the Whites at the Casa del Monte apartment building. Stahlman then turned to the issue of bruises.

STAHLMAN: Then when did you next see the defendant, Burmah White?

ANDERSON: A few minutes afterwards, in the Apartment 18.

STAHLMAN: Did you observe a bruise on her face?

ANDERSON: I did not observe it at that time. I observed it later on, at our office in the City Hall.

STAHLMAN: Did you hear a conversation at any time in which that bruise was discussed?

FRANCIS: May I have a "yes" or "no" answer to that?

ANDERSON: Yes.

STAHLMAN: Who was present at that conversation?

ANDERSON: Well, there was the defendant, Captain [S. J.] McCaleb, myself, and I believe Chief Taylor and Inspector Slayton and several other officers. I do not quite recall who all were there.[15]

STAHLMAN: State the conversation.

ANDERSON: Captain McCaleb says, "I notice a black and blue spot on your forehead."

At this, Francis objected, but Stahlman insisted that the defense first brought up the subject of bruising. Though this line of questioning seemed beneficial to Burmah because it showed that police had noticed bruising on her, it was dangerous territory for the defense. Francis did not want other things said at the police department to be allowed into the courtroom because, ultimately, the most damning words about Burmah probably came from Burmah herself.[16] But later, Francis was able to carefully cull more information from Anderson about the bruising: "Now, you say that you did not notice the bruises on Burmah White until after you had gotten down to the police station?" "Well," the officer replied, "I had not really had a good chance to look at her—that is, close up—until we got to the station." Francis, likely exasperated at this point, asked Anderson if he was denying that he saw bruising on Burmah. Anderson finally clarified that he most certainly did see a large bruise but that it was obviously old, because it was no longer black and blue but rather shades of yellow.[17]

Still, Stahlman was able to introduce portions of conversation that Anderson remembered having with Bergeron and Burmah in a police car to and from her grand jury appearance on September 13, 1933. According to Anderson, Bergeron asked Burmah if she was glad to get the whole ordeal off her chest, and that she said yes. Anderson asked her, "How did you ever expect to get by, using this same car, with the same license plates, right along?" The blonde suspect allegedly said, "Well, Tom wanted to get rid of it [but] I did not want to give it up." She continued, according to Anderson, "I could go around a corner 50 miles an hour and all the tires would stay on the pavement." "Weren't you afraid when you went out, knowing that those license numbers were broadcast to every radio car?" Anderson asked. "Well," Burmah supposedly replied, "on that Western Avenue job, we drove straight down Western Avenue and nobody ever bothered us. The other day, I drove it out to Santa Ana, to see my mother, and drove it back, without being bothered."[18]

Stahlman recalled Officer Bergeron to the stand. He reiterated verbatim what Anderson said regarding Burmah's confidence that she loved the Chevrolet coupe enough to risk getting caught, and that she loved how it took corners at 50 miles an hour. Stahlman asked the officer if she said anything else. She did, Bergeron said. "The guy who should have been arrested," Burmah said to him, "was the fellow who owned the

Graham-Paige" that she and Tom had stolen in their first job. "Why?" asked Bergeron. Burmah said that while she was making her getaway "she very nearly had a wreck because of faulty brakes."[19]

On October 31, 1933, right after the testimony of Leslie Bartel, one of the White's victims, the prosecution called its last witness for their case, J. Arthur Donato, manager of the Casa del Monte apartments. Both Stahlman and Cooper questioned Donato. They showed him some photographs and asked whether he had seen Tom and Burmah White between the 16th and the 31st of August of that year. Francis interjected, wondering what the prosecution's purpose was with his line of inquiry. "The first [crime] alleged in the indictment is the 16th," Cooper responded. "It is for the purpose of showing association in the renting of the garage." Bowron did not interfere, and Stahlman barreled ahead. "I object, your Honor, please," Francis said. "I understand that the purpose of this was to show a business transaction with this client in the renting of the garage." He even offered to stipulate to the renting of the garage for the sake of hiding Bartel's coupe, but Stahlman and Cooper insisted that they wished to have Donato testify, for reasons that soon became clear. Bowron finally overruled Francis's objection and allowed Stahlman to continue questioning the manager. Asking the same question several different ways, Stahlman established that Burmah did all the talking in her transaction with Donato and paid him for a week's rent. She gave him the name J. W. Allen as her own.

STAHLMAN: What was her general attitude towards you all of that time?

DONATO: Very pleasant and smiling. She had a pleasant smile. Everything seemed to be pleasant.

STAHLMAN: One other question. Did the man who accompanied her on the first visit to your place have any conversation with you?

DONATO: None whatever.

Here Francis tried to soften Burmah's image and depict her as someone who might have been naïve rather than someone who was comfortable facilitating crime:

FRANCIS: You say she was very pleasant and smiling?

DONATO: She was.

FRANCIS: Sort of a sweet, demure girl, was she?

DONATO: Pardon me?

FRANCIS: She was sort of a sweet, pleasant, demure girl? She was not a hardboiled, tough, "icy" blonde, was she?

DONATO: Well, I would not want to call anybody hardboiled without knowing it. I did not know anything about that.

FRANCIS: She did not impress you as being that way, did she?

DONATO: Pardon me?

FRANCIS: She did not impress you as being that sort of girl?

DONATO: A hardboiled girl?

FRANCIS: Yes.

DONATO: No, she did not impress me that way.

Attorney Francis took this opportunity to dampen the idea that Burmah acted without duress when she rented the garage for their stolen car:

FRANCIS: They paid from the 22nd to the 29th?

DONATO: To the 29th instant, the first time.

FRANCIS: Now, on that occasion there was a man with her?

DONATO: Yes, sir.

FRANCIS: Did he wear smoked glasses?

DONATO: Yes.

FRANCIS: And at all times while you were talking with her that man was present or within her sight, was he?

DONATO: That man was present. He was a few feet away all the time.

In fact, Francis established, Tom White was not more than a few feet away from his wife every time she conducted a transaction of any kind with this apartment manager—with the exception of one time, where she came to pay some overdue rent for the car.

FRANCIS: Here is the thing I have been trying to lead up to and why I have been trying to fix these dates: Do you remember at this time whether or not the last time she paid you 50 cents—do you recall or did you notice whether or not she had any bruises upon her face?

DONATO: Some rouge on her face?

FRANCIS: Bruises.

DONATO: Bruises?

FRANCIS: Yes.

DONATO: I recall particularly that I did not see any bruises on her face. I recall that her face was clear. I did not see a thing on her face, because I talked to her—well, three different times, and very closely. She was at my desk once, and of course, I treated her like I treat everybody. And I was very close to her, talking to her. And the man was a few feet away, and I could see her face. If there was a bruise there, I would have seen it.

FRANCIS: The last time you saw her, she didn't have a bruise on her face?

DONATO: No, not on her face.

FRANCIS: That is all.

CHAPTER 6

Trial, Part II

BETWEEN 11:00 P.M. AND 2:00 P.M. ON FRIDAY, OCTOBER 27, THE PROS-
ecution called a total of ten witnesses to testify on its behalf. Leslie Thomas
Bartel was first to take the stand. His friend Gertrude Host testified right
afterward. Originally from Kansas, the stocky blonde Bartel looked about
ten years younger than his thirty-two years. He was a life insurance agent
and proud of the fact that he had been taking care of his widowed mother
for almost his entire life. Because of his empathic nature, he did not hesitate
to take Host, his friend's mother, to the store when she, also a widow, needed
a ride on the evening of August 16, 1933. And she was no dull companion.
"Dr." Host taught transcendental meditation and astral projection at local
churches and kept company with a group that eventually founded a cult
based on the teachings of an obscure sixteenth-century French theologian.

At about 10:15 that evening of the 16th, Bartel drove Host back to
her fourplex on South Rampart Street, Los Angeles. Host got out of the
car first. "Do you want to come up upstairs?" she asked him, knowing
that he wanted to visit with her son. Tom and Burmah drove up. "I don't
remember what the first remark was," Bartel told the jury. "So I thought
perhaps it was someone who lived there or someone who knew Mrs.
Host, because it was in front of her home, and the thought of it being a
hold-up had never entered my mind. I completed locking the car just in
time to hear him say, 'Get back in there, sweetheart,' which was directed
at Mrs. Host.'" He then ordered Bartel to "shell out" as well, brandishing
a gun at both.

Stahlman asked Bartel to continue his narrative. Tom White, according to the salesman, forced Host to take off all her rings and other jewelry

and frisked Bartel, not believing that he had only four dollars in his possession. White demanded cash from Host, and when she protested that she had none, ordered her out of the car. Host had a cool head, if a daring one, and had thrown her purse onto the floor of the backseat of the automobile when White ordered her back in with his gun in her ribs. She also pushed her wristwatch up as high as she could on her arm, so White did not feel it when he felt for one. And because she heard White demand the keys to the car from Bartel, she made one more brave move: "Say, where is my coffee?" she asked loudly, to no one in particular. She ducked back into the car and retrieved her purse, which she had hidden under the backseat, then slipped it into her coat as though it were her grocery item and pulled the coffee out from her purse as though she had "found" it there in the car. White grabbed the coffee bag, ripped it open, and threw the contents in Host's face. Host ran as fast as she could up to her apartment door, and as she shakily put the key in the lock, she looked back and saw Burmah getting into the driver's side of Bartel's car. The criminal pair drove away in Bartel's green Graham Paige five-passenger sedan.

Defense attorney Francis cross-examined both Bartel and Host, asking many questions about White's ability to extract items from his victims with his right hand while brandishing a weapon in his left. His intent may have been to show that perhaps the victims were not in as much danger as they supposed, given that the criminal's hands were full. But as Stahlman showed on redirect, White was just as effective at terrorizing his victims with a gun in his left hand as he was with it in his right. And he established that Burmah White may have had just as much agency in this holdup as her husband did: "It was shortly after that that the defendant in this case walked up to the car; is that correct?" Stahlman asked Bartel, who confirmed that this was the case. After establishing that Burmah asked him to unlock the car, Stahlman asked for clarification:

STAHLMAN: But you recall that she did say, "Unlock the car?"

BARTEL: "Unlock the car and start it for me."

STAHLMAN: Were those the exact words she used, as near as you can recall?

BARTEL: As near as I can recall, she said, "Unlock this car and step on the starter."

STAHLMAN: Then what occurred?

BARTEL: Well, I turned the key in the car, in the lock, and stepped on the starter and got the motor running.

STAHLMAN: By the way when she told you to step on the starter and unlock it, what was the tone of voice?

BARTEL: I do not quite get what you mean?

STAHLMAN: What was the tone of voice that she used? Was it a commanding tone?

BARTEL: Yes.

Stahlman then repeatedly asked Bartel where Burmah was standing or sitting while Tom had a gun pointed at the two victims, how long Tom's attention was diverted from Burmah, and how far away he was from her. Defense attorney Francis finally interjected, saying the district attorney's questions were "constantly leading" and that it was not fair for him to describe and have the witness say "Yes" or "No." The judge overruled him. Francis objected again when Stahlman showed Bartel a police photograph of Tom that was at least five years old and asked if Bartel recognized the subject as the man who held him at gunpoint. Francis maintained that there was no foundation on which to admit it as evidence, but again, Bowron overruled him.

Francis knew exactly where Stahlman was headed with his examination of Bartel, and probably knew that he would continue trying to show that Burmah was under her own free will on many occasions with Tom.

"When Burmah White entered that machine," asked Francis of Bartel, referring to the car, "the gun was still cocked, wasn't it?" The witness conceded that it was. "And when Burmah White drove that machine off, did this man, Thomas White, sit beside her?" "In the front seat; yes, sir," the witness replied. Francis got Bartel to concede that Tom White could have held the cocked pistol on Burmah for any length of time after driving away, but the damage was already done.[1]

The next few witnesses called to the stand were employees of a Safeway grocery store on Tenth Street. One of them, butcher Luman Baker, was in back of the store, outside, not realizing that inside, Tom White was holding a gun on his coworkers and robbing them of cash. Baker watched a young blonde woman gunning a car in the back of the building:

> *Well, I kept watching the car, because the driver seemed to be very nervous, backing the car backwards and forwards, and sort of—well, moving in a radius of 10 or 12 feet all the time; the door was swinging open; she kept the motor racing, and kept glancing back into the stores. As I worked, I kept watching her, wondering just why all the nervousness. I knew she was not a customer of ours, and I wondered who she was. And the next thing I knew, someone jumped in the car and it raced away.*[2]

Baker could not remember whether he saw Burmah on August 31 or, as he said, October 5; the prosecution quickly dispatched this witness, but not before the defense ascertained that Baker thought Burmah seemed very agitated as she waited in the car for Tom.[3]

Francis managed to get the next witness, service station attendant C. E. McCurdy, to admit that he saw Tom holding his pistol low and loosely aimed at Burmah at times during their holdup of him. Stahlman tried to muddy this little detail: "Did you hear him direct any threat or demonstrate any menace toward the defendant, Burmah White, while he was there?" Francis's objection to this question was sustained.[4] McCurdy recounted how the Whites robbed him and his mother on the evening of August 26, 1933, using Bartel's maroon coupe:

They drove in, blocking the passageway for any car coming there, and so then I got off my stool and went out to see why they were block-ing the way. And at that time they started up again and drove in then [sic] opposite the pumps. So I walked around quickly, around the rear of it, around the rear of the car, and went up to [Burmah's] side, because I always go to the side where whoever is driving the car is. I stepped up to the window, and she looked up at me and said, "Step around to the other side. He wants to see you."

Stahlman then asked McCurdy a question that Francis strongly objected to but that Bowron allowed: "What was the tone of her voice when she told you that?" The witness said, "Well, it was not exactly what you would call 'hard-boiled.' It was just like a sharp little command; that is all."

McCurdy related what happened after that. The victim balked at giv-ing Tom his hard-won money—after all, this was the height of the Great Depression. But he relented when Tom pushed his gun into McCurdy's stomach, threatening to shoot him in the most painful way possible and, though he did not expressly say so, implied that McCurdy's mother might be next.

The Whites took everything McCurdy had earned that day: eleven dollars. But Francis did manage to use this testimony to illustrate that his client could be under the sway of someone, even if her victims did not hear Tom threaten her:

FRANCIS: And then this man, White, said to you, "Give me your money or I will blow your guts out." There was little doubt in your mind but what he meant it?

MCCURDY: No. I knew he meant it.

FRANCIS: Pardon?

MCCURDY: I was positive. That is why I opened the register. If I doubted it, I would not have opened the register.

FRANCIS: Not only the manner in which he said it, but the appearance of the man convinced you that he would not hesitate to do it. Is that correct?

MCCURDY: Yes.

Other witnesses, mostly store clerks who were robbed by the couple gave testimony. Bartel's coupe was clearly established as the one used to commit all these crimes after it was stolen on August 16, and the gun used by Tom to commit all these crimes was fairly proven to be identical to the one found on him the day of his death. It appeared that with some victims, Tom did not even bother to ask for money or jewelry but simply fired on them to stun or hurt them, allowing him to take anything he found off the person. Furniture salesman Clarence C. Lewis testified to his creepy ordeal the night of August 31, 1933, while climbing the stairs to his second-story apartment. After using the police photograph to have Lewis identify White as the man who ultimately shot at him, the prosecutor had Lewis describe White's attempt to hold him up:

COOPER: And, as you were going up the stairway, what happened?

LEWIS: I heard somebody following me up the stairway, and I had reached the first landing, and I turned around to see who it was, and I saw a man with a gun in his hand.

COOPER: I show you People's Exhibit No. 1, and ask you if you recognize that photograph as a photograph of a person you have seen before?

LEWIS: Yes, sir.

COOPER: You recognize that photograph as what person?

LEWIS: Thomas White.

The prosecution and Lewis established that White said nothing as he crept behind Lewis.

> COOPER: *And, when he got two steps below you, what did he say or do?*

> LEWIS: *He fired. He did not say anything.*

> COOPER: *And did that shot take effect?*

> LEWIS: *It grazed the flap of my pocket and entered the wall.*

> COOPER: *Had you any motion or done anything before he fired that shot?*

> LEWIS: *No, sir.*

> COOPER: *What did you do after he fired the first shot, or what did he do after he fired the first shot?*

> LEWIS: *He reached for my pocket, and I swung on him.*

> COOPER: *And as you swung on him, what did he do?*

> LEWIS: *Fired again and jumped down the stairway.*

Lewis did not mention Burmah by name during this portion of his testimony, but he made it clear that a blonde woman had driven the getaway car. There were a couple of conclusions the jury could draw from Lewis's testimony. On the one hand, it showed Tom could and would fire his weapon any time he felt like it. On the other hand, it showed that she had ample opportunity to simply drive away in the car to safety any time she felt like it.[5]

It had already been a long day on Friday, October 27, 1933. Reporters eagerly scribbled down the continued testimony of Gertrude Host and that of several drug and grocery store clerks and gas station owners. Both the prosecutors and defense attorneys established that Tom White was a violent felon who threatened to kill many of his victims unless they handed over the paltry sums they possessed. Only two of the witnesses saw her face, but no one argued that it could be anyone except Burmah with Tom during their crime spree. A hush fell over the courtroom as the prosecution called Crombie Allen to the stand.

Allen was a confident speaker in addition to being a successful newspaper publisher. He endowed a Peace Oratorical contest at both Chaffey High School and Chaffey College in Ontario, California, and was the first president of the Ontario Rotary Club and a member of the Rotary International. At times, lawyers had to ask him to speak up, though they did so politely, knowing his neck still hurt.

At about ten o'clock on the evening of August 16, 1933, Allen related, he and Withington picked up his car at the University Club at USC. He drove until they got to the corner of Lafayette and Third then switched places in the auto so that Withington could take the wheel. The pair drove down toward Sixth Street then turned around and came back up the east side of Lafayette. Just as they stopped at a stop sign, a car suddenly appeared alongside them, seemingly out of nowhere. While they took note of the car, they didn't pay much attention to it. "I'd like to drive it around the block one more time," Withington said, hoping to get more practice in the newer vehicle, which was considerably more fun to drive than her ten-year-old one. "Well," Allen replied, "as soon as this car crosses the traffic, why, then you can drive around the block." But the car never moved, and a man got out of it. Perplexed, Allen said to Withington, "This man must live in this house. As soon as he gets in, why, you can start and drive around the block again." Instead of moving along, though, the man closed the eight feet between them and stuck his head through Allen's car window.

COOPER: And what did he say, if anything?

ALLEN: Well, he had a gun in his hand, and he leaned in the car window and he says something like this: "Shell out, sweetheart, and that goes for you too, Bo!"

COOPER: Now, on whose side of the car was he? Your side or Miss Withington's?

ALLEN: Miss Withington's.

COOPER: And what did you and Miss Withington do at that time?

ALLEN: Well, we both realized that is was a hold-up and we began to shell out.

COOPER: And did you observe Miss Withington take any money or any valuables from her person?

ALLEN: Well, at first I reached down in my pocket, and I remember I did not have any money that day, but I had got a check for $20.00 cashed and I had spent $2.00, and I had $3.00 in one pocket and $15.00 in the other. I gave him one little bunch of bills, and he said, "Come across! Haven't you any more?" I reached in and got the other bills. Then he was going to grab my wrist watch, and I started to take it off and handed it to him. And, of course, I was pretty busy with that, and I was not quite sure what she had done all together.

Allen plowed ahead, not letting emotion get in the way of rattling off what happened next, having committed every detail to memory even in the midst of danger:

ALLEN: But I saw her reaching, when he first called to us, down and getting her bag and handing it to him. But he waved it back seemingly, that he did not want the bag, he wanted what was in it. She started to open it, and was considerably agitated, of course, and the zipper stuck.

COOPER: One of those zipper bags?

ALLEN: Yes. And she could not get it open.

COOPER: *And then what happened?*

ALLEN: *Well, it was so soon after that that I don't know whether anything really happened, whether he said anything or not, particularly. But the first thing I knew—it was just a few seconds or a moment afterward—why, I either saw a flash or heard an explosion. It was so quick together I did not know what. But I immediately felt a sting in the back of my neck and I reached up and pulled my hand down, and it was all covered with blood. And then I realized that he had shot me, but I never dreamed, of course, that he had shot a woman. But I thought, "We will catch him now," because he started over toward the car.*

COOPER: *Pardon me. During all of this time do you recall whether or not the motor of the car was running?*

ALLEN: *Oh yes. There was somebody in it and the motor was running all the time.*

COOPER: *And were you able to tell at any time, that evening, whether it was a man or woman at the wheel?*

ALLEN: *I could not tell myself. I saw it was some person, but from our position I could not see directly. I thought, "I will memorize the number." When I saw him going toward his car, I began to repeat it. As near as I recall, it was something like "8–X–893."*

COOPER: *You are not sure of that number?*

ALLEN: *Well, [it was] something like that, because I put it down afterward. And I said that, over and over again. And then I heard Miss Withington say it, too, and I thought she was watching the car license [plate] also. But then I noticed that her voice was very weak, and I turned around and saw for the first time that she had been shot, too. I did not realize that at first. And she was just repeating it after me, instead of seeing it on the car.*

According to some newspapers, there was a collective hush in the courtroom, with onlookers realizing what horror Allen must have endured when he realized that his companion was merely parroting his words in an effort to stay semiconscious.

COOPER: Now, did you see then what happened to the man that had fired the shot?

ALLEN: Well, he went over and got in the car, and they drove off into the traffic.

COOPER: Well, did you then observe the condition of Miss Withington?

ALLEN: Yes. Her head was collapsed, like that (indicating forward motion).

COOPER: Where was she shot?

ALLEN: Well, it went through the—in front of the left eye, grazing it, and down back of the right eye, and then came over and went through the back of my neck and then lodged in the side of the car.

COOPER: Now, did you get the bullet, or did someone get the bullet in that car?

ALLEN: I think the police got it later.

COOPER: Now, what was the condition of the eyesight of Miss Withington prior to this occasion?

ALLEN: Very good.

COOPER: And have you seen her since?

ALLEN: I have.

COOPER: And what is the condition of her eyesight now?

ALLEN: Well, she is blinded.

Defense attorney Francis jumped up, objecting to Allen's conclusion of this as a witness. Bowron overruled this motion, agreeing with Cooper that the prosecution could use it later as a means to connect it to another argument. But in fact, she was blind and would be for life. One of Withington's doctors called to the stand earlier had described the damage from Tom White's bullet:

At that time she was the victim of a hold-up, a gun shot by a thug, the bullet entering the left eye, taking part of the left lower lid with it, cutting that eye, penetrating the nose internally and high up, entering the right orbit, damaging the right eye, and emerging through the right temple, fracturing the malar bone and the external and internal walls of those orbits.

She would not, in fact, be able to testify in the courtroom at all, owing to the ongoing carnage wrought by the shot:

It would endanger further hemorrhage into the eye and damage to the eye. Some time about a month after the injury there was another hemorrhage [that] took place into the eyeball, with very little provocation, showing the damage to the blood vessels, which would allow them to burst and to bleed on the slightest provocation. Any nervous disturbance or upset tends to promote or provoke a further hemorrhage.

Furthermore, said the doctor, Withington suffered from extreme mental and nervous shock, and he did not expect that she would ever recover from the mental damage already wrought; discussing the incident at all would be catastrophic, even if the jury was able to come to her apartment.[6]

Allen discussed his identification of Tom White at the morgue as the man who shot him and Withington. After this, George Francis cross-examined him:

FRANCIS: Miss Withington's occupation, at the time of this occurrence, was that of a school teacher, wasn't it, Mr. Allen?

ALLEN: Yes, sir.

FRANCIS: Now, you were parked on Third Street, were you, or had stopped, rather, on Third Street?

ALLEN: No, on Lafayette.

FRANCIS: On Lafayette?

ALLEN: Yes.

FRANCIS: And near the intersection of Lafayette and Third Street?

ALLEN: Right at the boulevard stop there.

FRANCIS: Which direction were you traveling in?

ALLEN: We were traveling north, I suppose. Yes, on the right side, going up toward Third Street.

FRANCIS: And you stopped on the southeast corner of Lafayette and Third Street?

ALLEN: Yes.

FRANCIS: And how far back from the intersection had you stopped?

ALLEN: Oh, I suppose maybe 10 or 15 feet.

FRANCIS: And at that point a car pulled across in front of you and parked alongside of the curb in front of you?

ALLEN: No; pardon me. It just drew up alongside of us and in front of us, but not directly in front of us. We were next to the curb, and he was like as if in the second lane, if there had been any lanes.

FRANCIS: In other words, the car remained in a position parallel to the position in which you were driving, but not directly in front of you?

ALLEN: And ahead, yes. That is right.

Francis asked Allen to reiterate both the distance he thought they were from the White car and also that he had identified Tom White at the morgue. Then Francis moved on to the car itself and the events leading up to the shooting:

FRANCIS: When did you first see the gun that you have just described?

ALLEN: Well, when he put his head in through—this new Ford is much lower than the old type—so he stooped down a little and put his head in and his hand with the gun.

FRANCIS: And put his hand in with the gun. Now, you have repeated all the conversation that you heard on that occasion, have you?

ALLEN: I am not sure whether it is all of it, but that was the general trend of it.

FRANCIS: That is substantially all you heard said on that occasion by anyone?

ALLEN: Yes.

FRANCIS: Now, at the time Miss Withington was endeavoring to open her zipper purse, you were busily engaged in an effort to take off your wrist watch. Is that correct?

ALLEN: Yes.

FRANCIS: And then you heard this blinding flash?

ALLEN: Just a little bit after that.

FRANCIS: A little bit after that?

ALLEN: Yes.

FRANCIS: Well, now, Miss Withington made absolutely no effort to resist this man, White, at all, did she?

ALLEN: Well, not that I noticed.

FRANCIS: She was busily engaged, trying with both hands to open her pocket book?

ALLEN: Well, I am not sure about that, but I assume she was—that is what she was trying to do.

FRANCIS: Well, there was nothing—no incident that occurred upon that occasion, that you can now recall, that occasioned this man, White, firing that gun point blank into her temple, was there?

ALLEN: Well, I don't know whether I should say that he thought perhaps that she had said something that made him impatient, or not.

FRANCIS: I mean you did not hear her say anything to him that made him impatient ... you did not see her make a gesture of resistance? You heard no outcry of alarm, which would tend to frustrate his attempt to rob her. There was no occasion for it, so far as you know?

ALLEN: No.

FRANCIS: That is all.

Francis's strategy in this line of questioning is not clear, but if it was similar to the rest of his defense, he was likely trying to show the jury that Tom White was prone to violent attacks without any provocation whatsoever and thus that Burmah would also be subject to the same kind of attack and fearful of him.[7] Cooper got up to question Allen, and his strategy was quite clear: Burmah would damn herself with her own words:

COOPER: Have you, since that hold-up, ever had a conversation with the defendant?

ALLEN: Yes, sir.

COOPER: And where did you have any such conversation with her?

ALLEN: In the District Attorney's office.

COOPER: Where in the District Attorney's office?

ALLEN: Just in the room there; I don't know.

COOPER: In somebody's office there?

ALLEN: Yes.

COOPER: On the sixth floor of this building?

ALLEN: Yes.

Cooper was taking his time leading Allen to the crux of the prosecution's point in this line of questioning, but it was important. In modern times, it would be cause for a judge to summarily dismiss testimony or even a witness for many reasons, but not at this time and place.

> *COOPER: Who was present at the time you had this conversation with Burmah White?*
>
> *ALLEN: Buron Fitts.*
>
> *COOPER: Anybody else?*
>
> *ALLEN: Well, there were a number of people there.*
>
> *COOPER: Now, was there any force, threats or violence used against her at that time to make her talk?*
>
> *ALLEN: No, sir.*
>
> *COOPER: Any offer of reward or hope of immunity extended to her?*
>
> *ALLEN: No, sir.*
>
> *COOPER: Were her statements free and voluntary?*
>
> *ALLEN: They seemed to be.*
>
> *COOPER: What did you say to her and what did she say to you on this occasion?*

Francis objected. This line of questioning, he said, would only serve to impeach his client. Cooper pushed back. Whatever Burmah said to Allen in that cramped district attorney's office could be considered an admission or a confession. Francis asked Cooper if he could ask the witness a question of his own; Cooper relented.

FRANCIS: Were those statements reduced to writing?

ALLEN: I beg your pardon?

FRANCIS: Were those statements reduced to writing? Was there a shorthand reporter present on that occasion?

ALLEN: I am not sure about that part of it.

Bowron overruled Francis's implied objection. "You may answer the question," he told Crombie Allen.

COOPER: Will you relate the conversation, please?

ALLEN: Well, I had always been mystified afterwards why he had . . .

COOPER: Pardon me, to save an objection. Will you please just state what was said? What did you say to her, and what did she say to you?

ALLEN: As I recall it, I asked her why he shot us, and I am not clear about this thing, because I have not thought much about it. But, as I recall it, she said that she had asked him, when he got back after holding us up, if he had had—what caused the shot, or something of that sort. And he said he had to—

COOPER: He said or she said?

ALLEN: He told her, so she said, that he had to shoot, "to scare them."

COOPER: And did you ask anything about your wrist watch at that time?

ALLEN: Yes. I asked her what had become of the wrist watch, and she said she did not know.

COOPER: Did Mr. Fitts have some conversation with her in your presence at that time?

ALLEN: Yes.

COOPER: In connection with this occasion?

ALLEN: Yes.

COOPER: What questions did he ask her in your presence, and what replies did she make?

ALLEN: I don't recall much about that now, because there was a good deal of conversation.

COOPER: All right. Was that the substance of the conversation that you had with her at that time?

ALLEN: Yes, sir.

Nick Steponovich was the last victim called for by the prosecution, though he was one of the first known victims of Tom and Burmah White. "Mr. Steponovich," Cooper asked, "what is your business or occupation?" Nick mumbled something, and Cooper reiterated his question. "I run a club, up in Reno," the witness finally replied a bit more loudly. Cooper asked him if anything unusual happened to him on the evening of August 16, 1933. After some prodding by the prosecution, Steponovich admitted he was idling in his gray Chevrolet coupe at North Kingsley Drive in Los Angeles.

COOPER: And were you at the wheel?

STEPONOVICH: Yes, sir.

COOPER: Who was with you in your machine at the time?

STEPONOVICH: A girl by the name of Miss East.

COOPER: Miss East?

STEPONOVICH: Yes.

Steponovich was dating a woman in Reno, but this was likely not why he was reserved. In fact, the thirty-five-year-old man was on probation in Nevada and was not supposed to have left the state. Federal agents had raided his establishment, the Alley Club, and found copious amounts of whiskey, gin, and rum. He was arrested and sentenced to three months in jail, avoidable if he paid a hefty fine and stayed out of trouble. His "nuisance" offense was extremely common and just a cost of doing business for club owners during Prohibition, but calling attention to himself was the last thing Steponovich wanted to do while in Los Angeles, ostensibly to visit his sick mother. Making things more uncomfortable for him, the Chevrolet coupe he was driving was not his own but rather that of a female friend in Reno.[8]

The prosecutor moved on, though he frequently chided Steponovich for speaking too quietly to be heard by the court reporter. He told the jury about Burmah White's jumping out of a Graham-Paige and climbing into his car while Tom White marched him and his companion up the sidewalk with a gun in their backs. Burmah pulled Steponovich's borrowed auto up to the three of them, at which point Tom ordered them to "Keep going." He jumped into the car with Burmah, and off they went.

The prosecution then called its last witness: Burmah Adams White.

Portrait of Burmah Adams White. Photograph used for a *Los Angeles Herald and Express* article dated September 16, 1933. *HERALD-EXAMINER* COLLECTION/LOS ANGELES PUBLIC LIBRARY

Portrait of Thomas White. Photograph used for a *Los Angeles Herald and Express* article dated September 16, 1933. *HERALD-EXAMINER* COLLECTION/LOS ANGELES PUBLIC LIBRARY

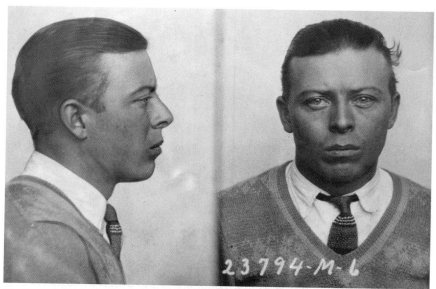

Photograph caption dated September 7, 1933, reads: "White, shown in this photo, fired at the heroic officers who trapped him with the gun which shot Crombie Allen, publisher, and blinded Cora Withington, school teacher, for life."
HERALD-EXAMINER COLLECTION/LOS ANGELES PUBLIC LIBRARY

Above: Photograph caption dated September 7, 1933, reads: "Here is the end of the trail for Thomas N. White, described by police as the 'rattlesnake' bandit, who shot down his helpless victims 'for no reason at all.' This photo shows his body in the shadowy hallway of a South Coronado Street apartment house where he was felled by two straight shooting police officers, Detective Lieutenants Arthur Bergeron and B. G. Anderson. White fired first, but as Bergeron said: 'He turned yellow and missed us.'" This is the apartment building at 236 South Coronado Street. *HERALD-EXAMINER* COLLECTION/LOS ANGELES PUBLIC LIBRARY

Facing page bottom: This photo was printed in the *Los Angeles Herald and Express*, September 18, 1933. The caption reads: "Photo, taken at the scene looking south on Occidental Boulevard from Third Street, shows a re-enactment of a holdup in which a bandit shot Crombie Allen, civic leader, and Cora B. Withington, teacher. As Miss Withington stopped the car for the Third Street crossing, the bandit car came along side, a gunman jumped out and ran to the auto. After robbing her and Allen, he ruthlessly fired when they said they had no more money. Doctors said she may be blinded for life." FRANK BENTLEY, *HERALD-EXAMINER* COLLECTION/LOS ANGELES PUBLIC LIBRARY

Photograph caption dated September 9, 1933, reads: "This dramatic photo shows Burmah White, icy blonde widow, appearing in a police 'showup' last night before a score of victims of the slain 'rattlesnake' bandit, Thomas N.[*sic*] White. With a group of girl police department employes [*sic*], mostly blondes, and the slain bandit's sister, Violet Dillon, the icy blonde paraded before the victims with a sneer on her face. Suddenly a woman in the audience clutched a police-man's arm. 'That girl,' she whispered pointing to Burmah White, 'is the one who drove the car for the bandit that robbed me.' Then another woman and two men pointed out the girl as the bandit's aide. The White girl is indicated by arrow and Mrs. Dillon, who had no connection with the bandit's activities, is at the extreme left." This "showup" took place in the Homicide Department at City Hall. *HERALD-EXAMINER* COLLECTION/LOS ANGELES PUBLIC LIBRARY

Photograph caption dated September 9, 1933 reads, "In this picture the body
of White, whose 20-night reign of terror was ended by two police bullets, is
being viewed by a group of robbery victims in an attempted identification. Many
of them recognized him. Yesterday Crombie Allen, publisher, who was wounded
at the same time the rughless bandit blinded Cora Withington, school teacher,
said: 'Yes, that is the man. It serves him right.' As a result District Attorney Fitts,
convinced that the evidence is positive, is preparing to mete out swift justice to
White's alleged 'moll.'" Here White lies in state at Edwards Bros. Colonial Mortuary, located at 1000 Venice Boulevard. *HERALD-EXAMINER* COLLECTION/LOS ANGELES
PUBLIC LIBRARY

Facing page top: Photograph caption dated September 7, 1933, reads: "This photo shows the slain gunman's 19-year-old blonde bride, Burmah Adams White, being questioned by officers who disguised themselves in mechanics' overalls to trap the couple after a relentless search. Today the girl, who was alleged to have accompanied White on his wanton raids, announced that she was ready to give the 'lowdown.' The officers above are, left to right, Detective Lieutenants Arthur Bergeron, W. C. Burris, Harry Maxwell and G. B. Anderson." *HERALD-EXAMINER* COLLECTION/LOS ANGELES PUBLIC LIBRARY

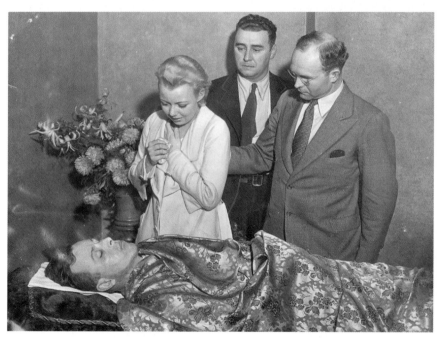

Photograph caption dated September 9, 1933 reads, "This photo shows the cold-eyed blonde viewing bullet-riddled body of Thomas N. White, her husband of five days, who was trapped and killed by detectives last Wednesday after a 2-night reign of terror. With her are her attorney, Donald Mackay, at left, and Detective Lieut. Leroy Sanderson. She haughtily walked into the morgue and posed with icy indifference, then like an actress going into a 'sob scene' she managed to sniffle a bit." Upon his death, White was taken to Edwards Bros. Colonial Mortuary, located at 1000 Venice Boulevard. *HERALD-EXAMINER* COLLECTION/LOS ANGELES PUBLIC LIBRARY

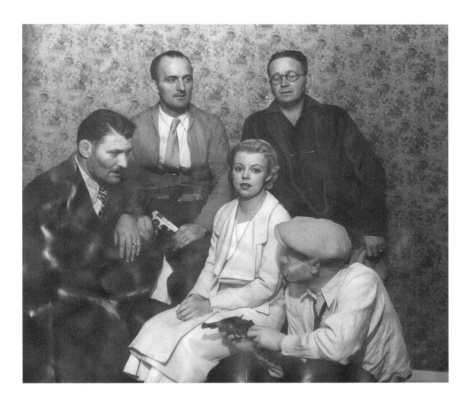

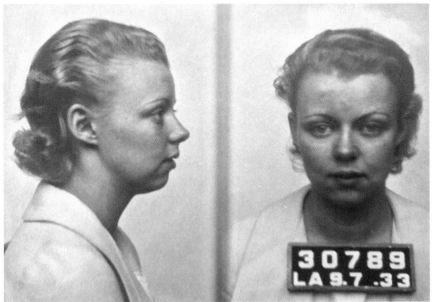

Burmah White's booking photo. The image has deteriorated over time, but with a close look, a large bruise can be seen on her forehead. COURTESY BURRIS FAMILY

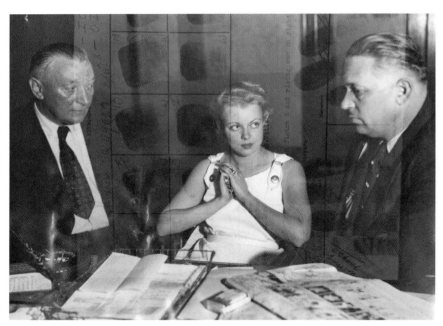

Burmah White with Chief of Detectives Joseph Taylor, left, and Captain of Robbery Detail S. J. McCaleb. Photograph dated September 16, 1933.
HERALD-EXAMINER COLLECTION/LOS ANGELES PUBLIC LIBRARY

Photograph caption dated September 9, 1933, reads: "Staring and smirking at the witnesses, Burmah White, blonde widowed bride of the slain 'rattlesnake' bandit, is pictured by the 'candid camera' as she appeared at the inquest. In center is Policewoman Lula Lane guarding the girl, and at right is Violet Dillon, the slain bandit's sister, who broke down and wept."
HERALD-EXAMINER COLLECTION/LOS ANGELES PUBLIC LIBRARY

Photograph caption dated September 8, 1933, reads: "Not long ago the girl was a pretty brunette student at Santa Ana high school. Then she bleached her hair, changed her face and even her disposition and became the bride of a paroled convict, who is alleged to have shot his victims for no reason at all."
HERALD-EXAMINER COLLECTION/LOS ANGELES PUBLIC LIBRARY

Photograph of the Adams family, left to right: J. A. Adams, Pearl Adams, Jo Louraine Adams, and Burmah Adams White. Photograph dated October 20, 1933.
HERALD-EXAMINER COLLECTION/LOS ANGELES PUBLIC LIBRARY

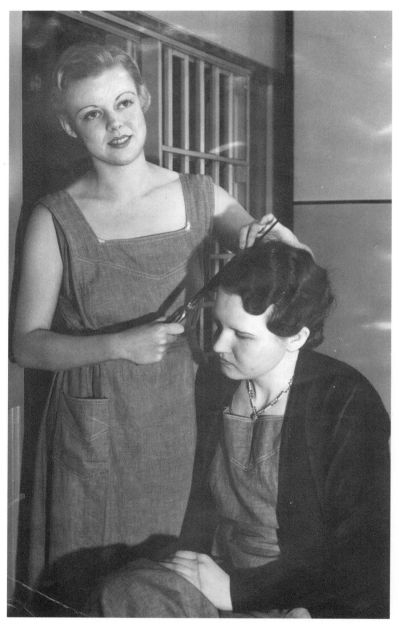

Los Angeles Herald and Express photograph caption dated September 18, 1933, reads: "Before Burmah White became the 'moll' of Thomas N. White, slain 'rattlesnake' bandit, she attended a beauty culture school and learned to dress hair. This photo shows her 'dolling up' one of her jail companions, Ruth Dollins, in preparation for the latter's appearance in court on a check charge." *HERALD-EXAMINER* COLLECTION/LOS ANGELES PUBLIC LIBRARY

Photograph caption dated October 20, 1933, reads: "Burmah White, 'icy blonde' widow of the slain 'rattlesnake bandit,' Thomas White, is pictured as she appeared in court today and had her trial on robbery charges continued until next Thursday. The case was postponed by Superior Judge Fletcher Bowron because of the illness of the girl's attorney. The prisoner maintained her cold attitude when brought from the county jail to court." *HERALD-EXAMINER* COLLECTION/LOS ANGELES PUBLIC LIBRARY

Photograph caption dated December 7, 1933, reads: "Taking along her tennis racket, indicated by arrow, Burmah White, convicted accomplice of the slain 'rattlesnake' bandit, is pictured when she left for the new state women's prison at Tehachapi today. At the new prison women live in bungalows and enjoy sports. The girl bandit is shown in custody of Deputy Sheriff H. M. Dennison and Nettie Yaw." *HERALD-EXAMINER* COLLECTION/LOS ANGELES PUBLIC LIBRARY

CHAPTER 7

Trial, Part III

ON OCTOBER 31, 1933, GEORGE FRANCIS CALLED HIS FIRST WITNESS for his defense of Burmah White. Pearl May Adams took the stand.

The attorney peppered Mrs. Adams with perfunctory questions about Burmah's growing up in Santa Ana and established that Burmah had gone through public school and worked at a soda fountain after school until she dropped out of Santa Ana High and received her cosmetician license in 1932. The first time Pearl met Tom White, she said, was around the 11th of August 1933. She was having trouble with a lock on the door to the family's rented apartment; Burmah called upstairs for Tom, who came down to fix it.

"Now," Francis asked, "from the time when you first met Mr. White, which you say was around the 11th day of August, until the date which I have just mentioned, the 6th day of September, did you notice any change come over your daughter, Burmah Adams White?"

George Stahlman leaped to his feet. "Just a moment! Object to that. It calls for a conclusion on the part of the witness. Incompetent, irrelevant and immaterial." (This is a commonly used phrase by a trial attorney to indicate that he or she believes the question is not about the issues in the trial or the witness is not qualified to answer.) Bowron sustained his objection. Francis found another way to ask Mrs. Adams to help him lay a foundation to show her daughter's state of mind during August and September.

"You had an opportunity before the 11th day of August to observe the conduct of your daughter, did you not?" Pearl agreed that she had and added that she and her daughter were always very close. "If you noticed any change in her general demeanor," Francis continued, "or in the general conduct or in the attitude of your daughter, subsequent to the 11th day of August, what it had been prior or shortly prior to that date, will you kindly tell us?"

Once again, Stahlman objected to this approach, and finally, after a lot of legal wrangling among Francis, Stahlman, and Bowron, the judge concluded that Francis's question would produce a conclusion by the witness that would not be fair and accused him of grandstanding. Still, Francis plowed ahead, determined to make his point:

Not under the reflection that I am attempting to make a speech, your Honor please. I am talking to the Court in good faith, trying to reach an understanding with this Court, trying to find a means of determining, your Honor please, one of the issues in this case. It appears to me quite clear, and it must be apparent to the Court, that the only defense this defendant has, and the only defense that will be urged by her, is the one pertaining to her frame of mind. One of the issues in this case is the condition and the frame of mind, as to whether or not she acted voluntarily, and as to whether or not she acted as a free agent. I believe, as your Honor pleases, that any change, any radical abrupt change in the general conduct, the general attitude and the general demeanor of this witness, immediately after she met that man, Tom White, which is a radical change from her conduct and her demeanor and her frame of mind, as evidenced by her conduct, is evidence, if your Honor pleases—or evidence, at least, in support of the fact we intend here to prove, that this defendant acted not as her natural, normal, free self, but acted under the threats and the violent coercion of the man, Tom White. Now if it is not proper for me to prove that, why, we can dispense with this witness in rather short order and that will settle the question.[1]

This speech set off another round of legal wrangling among prosecution, defense, and bench, so Francis ultimately capitulated and promised the court that he would try to "get the horse before the cart."

FRANCIS: *Now, Mrs. Adams, you were in the apartment, which you have described to us, on the day of September the 6th, were you?*

MRS. ADAMS: *Oh, yes.*

FRANCIS: *And you were there at the time of the arrest of your daughter, Burmah Adams White, was made, were you?*

MRS. ADAMS: *I was.*

FRANCIS: *At that time did you notice any scars or bruises upon the body or the face of your daughter?*

MRS. ADAMS: *I did.*

FRANCIS: *When had you first noticed those scars?*

MRS. ADAMS: *On the night of—let's see—say the—the last day of August, the 31st, I guess. The night of the 31st of August.*

FRANCIS: *Will you describe them to us, please?*

MRS. ADAMS: *A large bump on her forehead, and her—one arm—I believe it was her right arm—was bruised from the elbow up to the shoulder.*

FRANCIS: *What sort of bruises did you observe on her arm?*

MRS. ADAMS: *Well, just black marks.*

FRANCIS: *How many of them, and what were they?*

MRS. ADAMS: *Well, I don't know. From her shoulder down to her elbow was bruised, in spots. I don't know how many there were.*

FRANCIS: And those bruises were noticed again on the 6th day of September. Is that correct?

Stahlman asked to see the photographs. While he examined them, Francis asked Mrs. Adams if the images reflected the bruises she observed on her daughter. She said they did insofar as positioning and size but that she knew them to be "more pronounced" in person. Francis then called her husband and Burmah's father, Joseph Adams, to the stand. He reiterated the fact that the family had fallen on hard times in recent years and thus Burmah had to leave school to look for work.

Joseph Adams also told the court that he did not meet his daughter's fiancé until August 20, 1933, and that he observed that Tom White rarely left Burmah's side when he, Joseph, was around. He did not see Tom more than a few times before the pair married. Francis asked Mr. Adams about what he noticed on September 1, his daughter's wedding day:

FRANCIS: And did you notice the condition of your daughter's face, as to the bruises or scars, before the wedding on that day at that time?

ADAMS: I certainly did.

FRANCIS: Will you tell us what it was, please, Mr. Adams?

ADAMS: Well, there was quite a lump on her forehead, for one thing I noticed. And there were several bruises on her arm; and I noticed a bruise up here, around her chest. Just how many, I don't remember, but there were several of them, and they were not very small, either.

Adams went on to describe the various bruises he noticed on his daughter during the time she "went with" Tom White, especially one in the middle of her forehead when she was arrested and one that seemed to circle part of her neck. Francis recalled Mrs. Adams to ask her more questions about specific bruises on her daughter, specifically about the bad bruise across her pelvic bone that Burmah told her she got while surfing, one across her back, and several on her arms and her neck. She also discussed Burmah's injured ankle. None of these, she said, seemed "fresh." She estimated they had been there for a few days. At this point, Francis tried very hard to introduce the notion that Burmah finally broke down and admitted to her parents where her injuries had really come from, but Stahlman successfully blocked this, objecting that anything Burmah said after her arrest would be in the nature of a self-serving declaration.

After lunch on this Halloween Day of 1933, reporters jostled for space and scratched loudly with their pencils as Burmah Arline Adams White was called to the stand. She related her employment record since residing in Los Angeles off and on since 1931. It was, by anyone's standards, spotty at best. She admitted working on occasion for three or four different employers and did not offer any details on them. But this was the height of the Great Depression—many people had spotty employment records—and this information did not seem concerning to either the prosecution or defense. What Francis did try to do, however, is pluck out Burmah's inherent goodness by her responsible behavior at one of her most consistent jobs, that of cosmetician at Mildred Juhnke's beauty parlor at 7715 South Central Avenue.

FRANCIS: And during that time you worked in this beauty parlor, you say you were in charge of it, left there alone, were you?

COOPER: To which we object as immaterial.

FRANCIS: It is preliminary.

COOPER: I will say this, may it please the Court: At this time, that while it is preliminary, if counsel wants to open up the life history of this young lady, so long as he will give us the same opportunity to show other facts, we won't have any objection. But I do not feel that he should go into immaterial matters and then we be precluded from cross-examining. So, therefore, I will stand on the objection, that this kind of examination is immaterial.

Bowron allowed Francis and Burmah to continue framing her life before it was interrupted by Tom White. A woman whose hair she had worked on at Mildred Juhnke's asked the young blonde to join her and her boyfriend at Sebastian's Cotton Club. Burmah insisted she had no idea what Tom's occupation was. And she insisted that she did not want to drive the car when they held up Allen and Withington, but Tom forced her to do so *at the point of a gun*. With Francis's guidance, she gave her own rambling version of the events of their crime spree beginning August 16:

> *I was walking down the street with Tom White. And we approached the car that had just parked at the curbing, and which I found out later Mr. Bartel and Mrs. Host were occupying. They had just pulled to the curb, and we were directly parallel with the car when Tom White said, "Just a minute," and walked over to the car. At the time, I got just a glimpse of a flash of a gun. I stood there for a few minutes while he was talking to the people. What he said, I don't know. I was standing on the sidewalk running parallel with the curb, about . . . well, from five to ten feet away from the car. I was, well, so frightened at the time I couldn't move; I couldn't say anything. Tom was standing there with a gun turned on these people and I stood stock still. Mrs. Host stepped out of the car and brushed by me, and Tom White turned to me and said, "Get in the car," and flashed his gun—waved his gun at me. I entered the car, and he told me to start the car. And, either through fright or lack of knowledge of the car, or some reason, I could not seem to start it. I asked Mr. Bartel to start the car for me, which he did. Tom got in, still holding his gun in his hand. He told me to step on it, get out of the neighborhood, and keep my mouth shut, or he would give it to me.[2]*

Why, then, Francis asked, did she not simply leave the scene when she became aware that it was a holdup?

WHITE: I was afraid to move.

FRANCIS: Why were you afraid?

WHITE: Because Tom White was standing there with a gun in his hand and he could see me.

FRANCIS: And why did you enter the machine and drive away with Tom White?

WHITE: Because I was afraid he would shoot me if I did not. I was afraid he would kill me.

For the next hour and a half, Burmah relayed virtually the same story for each of the holdups she and Tom perpetrated. Attorney Cooper didn't object until Francis suddenly deviated from this line of questioning:

FRANCIS: Did Tom White ever, in connection with the threats [that] you have related, resort to any physical violence upon your person?

COOPER: To which we object unless it is confined to the time that she was actually out on the job, under the cases heretofore cited. . . . I do not mean to concede that it did happen, but if at some other time and place, other than when she was actually out on the job, she was struck or shot or hit over the head with a club, it would be absolutely immaterial; it would be no defense to these particular charges, under the cases which your Honor has before you—unless the violence was used or threatened on the job.

Judge Bowron overruled Cooper's objection . . . twice. Francis tried again to get Burmah to relay her depictions of physical abuse by Tom White, but Stahlman jumped in and tried again to stop her from doing so. And for a third time, Bowron overruled the prosecution's objection. Francis asked his client again to tell the courtroom what her husband did to her at various times that second half of August 1933:

BURMAH: He beat me horribly, that day.

FRANCIS: He beat you horribly?

97

BURMAH: Yes, sir. I was crying—

FRANCIS: Did he hit you around the head?

BURMAH: Not that [particular] day, no.

FRANCIS: When did he do that?

BURMAH: I think the 31st of August.

FRANCIS: And were any of these beatings, which you have been talking about, the result of your objecting to accompanying him or associating yourself with him after you discovered what his activities were?

One can imagine both Cooper and Stahlman leaping to their feet when Francis asked this last question of Burmah. They objected to it, and even after Bowron sustained it, they asked to approach the bench with all counsel. That discussion isn't recorded, but Francis was able to rephrase his line of questioning, which still elicited objections from the prosecution. Francis was undeterred:

FRANCIS: When was the last time Tom White struck you?

BURMAH: I believe it was the night before the 1st of September.

FRANCIS: And did he tell you why he was striking you?

BURMAH: Yes, sir.

FRANCIS: Why did he say—or what did he say as the reason for his beating you up on that occasion?

BURMAH: To make doubly sure that I would not hesitate about going ahead with the ceremony, the following day, the wedding ceremony.

FRANCIS: Did he tell you why he administered any of these other beatings upon your person?

BURMAH: At the time?

FRANCIS: Yes.

BURMAH: What did he have to say about those?

Burmah recalled that Tom told her she could not possibly get away, that he would never let her. He told her she would get a beating like the one he administered the night before their wedding if she ever tried it . . . that from that time on, "I should know who was boss."[3]

Burmah then relayed the events that she told *True Story* magazine: When Tom returned to their apartment the evening of August 16, 1933, he became enraged when he saw the second dinner plate and ashtray that belonged to Burmah's would-be beau from high school. "He said he would put me in a position where I could not see anybody else—where I would not want to see anybody else." And it was at this time, she said, that she got the first inkling that Tom was a criminal. "You don't know how I am making my money," he told her. "Maybe you think I have plenty. Well, I have; here it is!" and pulled out a gun. "Well, I need money, and I need help, so I am going to use you," Burmah recalled.

Cooper cross-examined Burmah. It did not go well for her case. The teen was cagey about when she moved to the Casa del Monte apartments, whether Tom already lived there or not, and why she used the pseudonym Alexandria Leader to rent an apartment there—things that would be obvious even to the most distracted person. She insisted that Tom was a perfect gentleman and that she had no idea what he did for a living—after two months of dating—until the evening of August 16, when he became enraged at the thought of her dating another man and purportedly forced her to become his accomplice in crime.

Cooper's questions to Burmah during this first cross-examination were undoubtedly meant to determine that she was less than forthcoming about details, but as a whole, the line of inquiry gave the impression that if she was a victim of Tom's, she was also a "stepper"—a loose girl:

COOPER: *Didn't you know that he was living there at that time?*

BURMAH: *I don't know that he was, no.*

COOPER: *What is that?*

BURMAH: *I don't know that he was.*

COOPER: *Now, on the night of the 16th of August, what were your feelings toward Tom White?*

BURMAH: *At what time during the evening?*

COOPER: *Well, before he got mean.*

BURMAH: *Oh, I loved him.*

COOPER: *And had he up to that time expressed his affection toward you?*

BURMAH: *Yes, sir.*

COOPER: *In other words, it was mutual, then, at that time?*

BURMAH: *Supposedly so.*

COOPER: *All right; you thought so?*

BURMAH: *Yes.*

COOPER: *Now, on the night of the 16th of August, you had been out with somebody else?*

BURMAH: No; I had had an old school mate for dinner in my apartment.

COOPER: What is that?

BURMAH: I had had an old school mate of mine for dinner.

COOPER: And who was that?

BURMAH: I couldn't tell you his last name. His first name was Al somebody.

COOPER: What? Al something?

BURMAH: Al something; I don't remember.

COOPER: An old school mate of yours?

BURMAH: An old school mate of mine from Santa Ana.

COOPER: You had known him for years and years?

BURMAH: Quite.

COOPER: What was his last name?

BURMAH: I did not say.

COOPER: You do not know?

BURMAH: I do not know.

COOPER: What school did you attend with him?

BURMAH: The Santa Ana High School.

COOPER: *Was he in some of your classes?*

BURMAH: *Yes, sir.*

COOPER: *How did you happen to get in touch with Al?*

BURMAH: *I beg your pardon?*

COOPER: *How did you come—how did he come to come to your apartment, that night?*

BURMAH: *He has been working in Santa Ana, and when I go home, I quite frequently see him.*

COOPER: *And you do not know his last name?*

BURMAH: *I do, but I don't remember it.*

All Burmah could recall about Al was that he worked at Alpha Beta Market on Fourth Street in Santa Ana. Cooper and Stahlman concluded that there was simply no person named Al and that she was using this fictional person to establish her basis for defense. Nonetheless, they indulged the idea that Tom was enraged by her trying to cheat on him and pushed her out of the apartment building at gunpoint for two blocks, until they came upon Leslie Bartel and Gertrude Host. At one point, Cooper and Burmah discussed whether she had told Bartel, "Start the car for me, please," or "Start that car and be damned quick about it!"[4]

This last quibble—exactly how Burmah told Bartel to start the car—seems like an innocuous detail in a trial of such magnitude. But this trial was full of these split hairs because not only was Burmah's attitude ripe for appraisal but the defense was doing its best to defend her without the benefit of time to prepare and time to depose the witnesses. When Stahlman recalled Bartel to the stand to discuss exactly how Burmah told him to start the car, he asked, "Mr. Bartel, I understand there was some conversation that you had with the defendant, Burmah White, at the time of the hold-up, which you did not testify to on your previous appearance on the stand. Is that correct?" Before Bartel could relate this, Francis jumped up and objected, insisting that it was improper to reopen a line of questioning during redirect examination. Bowron intervened, and Bartel admitted that he had never been asked this question by the prosecution, and he just now remembered that it happened. Bowron overruled Francis's objection and let Bartel answer: "And she said, 'Come on! Quit stalling and start this car and start it damned quick!'" Again, Francis objected, exasperated:

FRANCIS: Whom have you talked to about this case since you took the witness stand last, Mr. Bartel?

BARTEL: In what way do you mean? Outside of the court room?

FRANCIS: In any way, Mr. Bartel.

STAHLMAN: Object to that as being absolutely immaterial.

It was not immaterial, and Bowron knew it. He overruled Stahlman's objection.

BARTEL: Well, is it necessary to mention names of anyone whom I have talked to, your Honor?

BOWRON: Counsel has a right to know whether this conversation has been suggested to you by someone else, after you left the witness stand, and he has the right to know whom you have been talking to since you gave your testimony last.

Bartel hemmed and hawed a bit. At this, Bowron grew impatient and directed him to say exactly with whom he had discussed what Burmah supposedly said when instructing Bartel to start the car. He finally admitted that he brought it to the attention of the prosecuting attorneys . . . after he had already testified against Burmah earlier in the trial. In other words, he changed his testimony to make the teen sound more menacing. This admission forced the prosecution to have Bartel repeat his entire recollection of his ordeal with the Whites, which may have served to simply remind the jury of her complicit behavior.

Cooper and Stahlman then queried Burmah extensively about the holdups and shootings that Tom did, and tried hard to tie her to three or four other robberies, including that of diamonds from Miss Alma Fell at the Marbro Shop at 6311 Pacific Boulevard in Huntington Park, southeast Los Angeles. This incident and several others happened between August 10 and August 15, and it would have been a coup for the prosecution if Burmah would admit to them because it would show that she was not scared of Tom because of the Allen-Withington shooting. Though these other charges were eventually tossed out by the judge, the jury heard them, and the evidence was fairly damning: Not only did the victims identify Burmah and Tom as the perpetrators (and they had close-up contact with both), the car used was the same make and color Essex automobile that Pearl Adams owned and often loaned her daughter. Additionally, Burmah used to work at a beauty shop within half a mile of the Marbro Shop and would buy clothing there on occasion. Still, she adamantly denied having participated in these events.

The next round of testimonial skirmish between Francis, the prosecution attorneys, and Burmah seemed inconsequential at first, but it soon became obvious that the young defendant walked into a trap laid by her own words. It was not the first or last time she would do this.

"As a matter of fact," Cooper asked, "you had a number of interviews with newspaper reporters, to whom you gave your whole life story?"

"No, sir," Burmah replied.

Cooper approached the question from another angle.

"Did you at any time have any interviews with any newspaper men?"

"Yes. They were at Lincoln Heights Jail practically every morning, to see me."

"Did you ever tell any of them," Cooper continued, "that Tom White had threatened you?"

One can imagine Burmah relaxing in her seat, thinking that at last, the prosecution team could see how her husband forced her to do all these terrible things. "Yes, sir," she blurted out, too fast for her attorney to object.

"Just a moment," Francis jumped in.

"What is that?" Cooper asked. "Is there an objection?"

Francis knew exactly where Cooper was headed, and lamely attempted to ward it off by jumping up and telling the judge, "She had answered the question before I had an opportunity," he said. No sympathy or redirection from Bowron or Cooper.

COOPER: *Whom did you tell that Tom White had threatened you, before you saw a lawyer?*

BURMAH: *I don't remember.*

COOPER: *When did you first see a lawyer?*

Francis objected, but Bowron overruled him.

BURMAH: *I couldn't tell you. For a week after my arrest I couldn't possibly tell you how events came or in what order they came.*

COOPER: *Wasn't your mind free at that time?*

BURMAH: *Free? Free, but dazed.*

Cooper needled her more about her state of mind while in detention with the district attorney's office and the jail. Was her mind clear enough to write any letters? She did not recall writing any letters. Well, did she think clearly enough to write some notes? Yes. Yes she did.

COOPER: *And do you remember writing a note for Mr. Shambra, a newspaper reporter?*

BURMAH: *Yes, sir.*

After some procedural tussling, Cooper got his question in:

> COOPER: *Do you remember telling him that you were gambling for high stakes?*

> BURMAH: *Yes, sir.*

> COOPER: *What did you mean by that?*

> BURMAH: *I couldn't tell you.*

The damage was done, though. Her statement gave the impression that she had done some very bad things, and that her "not guilty" plea was a risky move she had to take because she had been *caught*.

⸻

Joseph Adams looked about twenty years older than his fifty-five years when he took the stand on October 31. His face was pinched and dark, and his large brown, doe-shaped eyes drooped with exhaustion. His suit hung from his already slim frame because he had not been able to eat well for nearly a month and a half due to the stress of his daughter's arrest and trial. Adams admitted to the jury he was dumbfounded at his elder child's choice of mate. Francis asked him to describe the event to the jury:

> *It was very unusual. To state it in my own words, it occurred to me at the time—I thought to myself, "My God! What is the matter with that girl?" And I thought, "Is she losing her mind?" She seemed sort of hysterical, and, to my way of expressing it, "jeery." She made some peculiar noises—some people would say, "Hysteria"—a halfway laugh and a halfway cry, as near as I can describe it, right in the ceremony.*

Did she, Francis asked Adams, "have that peculiar smile that is characteristic of her?" Stahlman objected. Francis asked again.

ADAMS: Well, it might have been a smile. I don't know what you could call it. It did not look like a happy smile, by any means.

FRANCIS: Some sort of contortion of her lips, was it?

ADAMS: Yes, sir.

FRANCIS: This conduct that you observed in your daughter upon that occasion—did you ever observe that before?

Stahlman objected to this, knowing where Francis was leading Adams.

ADAMS: Not exactly the same kind of conduct, but she had not been the same girl for three or four weeks, or I would say two or three weeks, at least. I had noticed it.

FRANCIS: What did you notice about her that led you to that conclusion?

ADAMS: Well, she seemed to be under a mental strain a good deal of the time. And at other times she was very irritable, which was not her usual conduct. And at other times she seemed to be in a deep study. We noticed it. My wife and I both commented about her, "What in the world is the matter with her?"

Joseph Adams noticed something else about his daughter about the middle of August. She'd started to bite her fingernails down to the quick, something she had never done because she took pride in keeping herself impeccably manicured so that her salon clients would know they were being treated by a professional. She chewed and chewed them, Adams maintained, from August 16 through the time of her arrest. He had never seen her do that before. Stahlman objected to the relevance of this information and could not help but make a pointed remark to Adams when he was allowed to: "You did not know," he said, "that during that period of time that you had observed your daughter and noticed that she was irritable, that she had been committing robberies, did you?" He had not.[5]

Cooper recalled Burmah to the stand for a scathing cross-examination. He grilled her for nearly an hour, forcing her to admit that there were plenty of opportunities for her to escape the clutches of Tom White if she wished to do so. Her mother had come to stay with her and spent at least five nights with Burmah and Jo in the apartment, at which time Tom would retire to his own rental upstairs. But still, Burmah maintained to Cooper, she was afraid for her own life and that of her family if she did not stay in the apartment:

COOPER: *And he told you that if you left at any time, why, he would kill your family?*

BURMAH: *I could not say in those words. The thought was there.*

COOPER: *And you were afraid that he would carry out that threat and murder your family?*

BURMAH: *I was quite sure he would carry out his threats.*

COOPER: *You were sure; you were afraid that he would murder your mother or father or your little sister?*

BURMAH: *I was afraid that I would be jeopardizing their lives if I left.*

And yet, Cooper was able to elicit from the teen, she never told her mother or father or a single soul that she was in danger, even when she came with Tom to Santa Ana in the stolen maroon coupe to tell her family she was getting married:

COOPER: *Now, as a matter of fact, at the time you obtained your marriage license certificate, you and Tom came running across the street, and you had the marriage license in your hand and you were*

laughing and smiling, weren't you, as you came across the street, and
you showed it to this young lady, back here, this Violet Dillon, and you
got in the machine with Violet Dillon and you were happy?

BURMAH: I may have appeared so on the surface, for the benefit of
my mother, but I most assuredly was not.[6]

Later, near the end of the trial, the prosecution called Violet Dillon as
a rebuttal witness. She said that her brother and Burmah came out of the
courthouse "smiling and happy"; Cooper asked Dillon two more times
about how she perceived the teen's demeanor until Olin MacKay pleaded
with the judge to make Cooper stop asking the same question and calling for a conclusion. Still, almost all of Dillon's testimony was composed
of her assessment that Burmah was "smiling and talking" or "smiling and
happy" from dawn until dusk on her wedding day.

Finally, Cooper ended his line of questioning to Dillon. Francis jumped
in to ask Dillon if her brother was in her care as a parolee during the night-
marish weeks of August 16 to September 6, 1933. She agreed that he was.
Cooper saw an opportunity, and he took it. Tom "was released, however,
before the 16th of August, was he not?" "He was released in April," Violet
responded, likely nodding her head in the affirmative. "And it was at that
time that he first was released to your care and custody?" Yes, she answered.
The inference was not lost on the jury: Violet Dillon may not have been
able to keep her brother in line the last three weeks of his life, but he had
not been caught doing anything violent until he met Burmah Adams.[7]

In all, the prosecution produced thirty-two witnesses for its case
throughout the trial, not counting Burmah Adams White, who was called
as a rebuttal witness for her own testimony. In all, the defense produced
five witnesses for its case, including Burmah. In addition to her parents,
her attorneys got William B. and Silva Casey to testify on behalf of the
teen they'd known as their across-the-street neighbor for seven years.
William was a mechanic for the Holly Sugar Corporation and, besides
being neighbors, had friends in common with Joseph Adams because of
their shared bakery ties. He and Silva attended the little wedding across
the street on September 1, 1933:

FRANCIS: Did you have an opportunity to observe the appearance of the defendant before that ceremony?

CASEY: I did.

FRANCIS: Did you notice any bruises or scars about her body?

CASEY: I did.

FRANCIS: Will you describe them to us, please, Mr. Casey?

CASEY: There were probably—I don't know just how many—five or six large black and blue marks on her right arm, between her shoulder and elbow.

Later, Casey's wife, Silva, described the bruises she and her husband noticed with a little more detail: "There was a large, black bruise mark on her right arm, somewhere between her elbow and shoulder. And there was a large, bruised, blue place on her forehead, up over her right eye, running up into her hair."[8]

FRANCIS: Now, you have known this defendant as a girl for a number of years, have you?

WILLIAM CASEY: Yes.

FRANCIS: Had an opportunity to observe her demeanor and her conduct?

CASEY: Yes, sir.

FRANCIS: When she was a girl in high school, in Santa Ana?

CASEY: Yes.

FRANCIS: Did you note, at the time of her marriage, anything that struck you as being unusual about her attitude or conduct?

Stahlman objected, stating this called for a conclusion of the witness. Bowron let the question stand.

CASEY: Well, she appeared to be very unhappy for a girl that was about to be married, and under a great mental strain and trying to control herself.

Francis finished his questions; Stahlman jumped in.

STAHLMAN: She appeared to be very unhappy, did she?

CASEY: Yes, she did.

STAHLMAN: What did she do that indicated to you that she was unhappy?

CASEY: Well, I don't believe, if I remember right, that the whole evening did I ever see the girl smile at her wedding.

Stahlman asked Casey how many people were at the wedding, perhaps trying to show that Casey could not possibly have watched Burmah's demeanor the whole time in such a crowded place. He veered away from this line of questioning when Casey said that everyone who was at the event was in the courtroom, pointing out all the guests and noting that only a baby or two were absent—about twenty people, including Burmah's family. Stahlman quickly asked Casey a question he knew would be vociferously objected to, and it was: "You did not know that for a period of several weeks previous to this wedding that she had been engaged in a number of robberies throughout the City of Los Angeles, did you?" After being chastised by defense counsel, Stahlman asked a simple question: "You know her parents?" He did. "She has quite a fine old father and mother, hasn't she?" Casey had to agree. Stahlman did not have to make it any more obvious: Burmah came from a good home, and there was no reason on earth for her to behave the way that she had.[9]

Francis called Captain S. J. McCaleb, head of the Robbery Division, to the stand. He quizzed McCaleb about the list of robberies with which he confronted Burmah about the night she was arrested—and the people on that list who could not identify Burmah as the woman who helped rob them.

FRANCIS: After she left your office, some newspaper reporters came into your office, did they not?

MCCALEB: Yes.

FRANCIS: And you told those newspaper reporters that she had not told you everything, that she was on the dope and when she got off the dope and her mind cleared up she would ask for more dope and you would probably be able to get all the information out of her, did you not?

MCCALEB: I did not.

FRANCIS: Did you not tell the newspaper reporters that she would not talk because she was full of hop?

MCCALEB: I believe that statement was made on the 6th day of September, not the 7th.

FRANCIS: Oh, you told the officers on the 6th day of September that she was full of hop?

MCCALEB: I did not tell the officers. I told the newspaper reporters that I thought she was under the influence of narcotics.

FRANCIS: Now, are you sure that you told the newspaper reporters that on the 6th day of September, and not on the 7th day of September?

MCCALEB: Positive.

FRANCIS: So when you saw her on the 6th day of September, she didn't bear a normal appearance—she was not collected?

MCCALEB: No, she did not appear to be normal on the 6th day.

FRANCIS: She appeared to be full of hop, did she?

MCCALEB: She appeared to have something the matter with her. I wouldn't say she was a normal person on the 6th.

If members of the jury thought Francis was splitting hairs with Captain McCaleb, they soon realized that the attorney established that anything Burmah told police on the day of her arrest was not reliable because she was probably drunk, on drugs, or both. But any gains made by establishing this notion were washed away when policewoman Marie Dinuzzo took the stand and discussed her version of events that took place on September 7.

"Were you present," Stahlman asked Dinuzzo, "at a conversation wherein a number of police officers were present, yourself, and Captain McCaleb, in which she was asked what she knew about the robberies, and then for some period of time repeatedly stated that she knew nothing about them?" She was. But Dinuzzo also testified that there was more to that conversation. After insisting she knew nothing about the robberies, Burmah—unbelievably—accepted a list of them from McCaleb and said, "I will show you which jobs I went on." She proceeded to check off with a pencil which "jobs" she participated in, and then—even more unbelievably—told the room of officers why she did them: "Yes, I got Tom to go with me on these robberies because my little sister needed treatment for her ears. . . . I committed the robberies with Tom to get money to pay for these treatments."[10]

Stahlman and Cooper recalled some witnesses from robberies that occurred before August 16, 1933. On Wednesday, November 1, 1933, at 2:00 p.m., Bowron told the jury to go home, get some rest, and be ready to begin deliberating over Burmah's future in the morning. On Monday, November 6, 1933, the jury's verdicts were read: Burmah Adams White was convicted of seven counts of robbery, one count of attempted robbery, and three counts of assault with a deadly weapon with intent to commit murder.

CHAPTER 8

Tehachapi

ON DECEMBER 6, 1933, A PHOTOGRAPHER FROM THE *LOS ANGELES Herald and Express* snapped a photo of Burmah on a platform at Union Station, flanked on one side by Deputy Sheriff H. M. Dennison and on the other by Deputy Sheriff Nettie Yaw. Burmah wore a dark velvet dress, and a suitcase rested at her feet. The image also showed a tennis racquet lying on top of her valise. The *Herald and Express* pasted a large, white arrow pointing at the racquet, in case it was not clear to readers that maybe this eminent inmate was going to have a life of leisure at the new women's state prison at Tehachapi.

Burmah's demeanor in newspaper photos belied her anxiety—or perhaps it revealed her internal denial—that she was headed to San Quentin prison to serve thirty years to life. After her verdict was read by the forewoman, Bowron made it clear that Burmah's actions served as an example of how too much pampering of young persons who violated the law could lead to a rise in criminal behavior:

We have heard much about the enlightened treatment of criminal tendencies where they develop early in life. But, despite reforms or reformers, or possibly because of them, we now have a younger generation growing into young manhood and young womanhood which evinces criminality to a far greater extent than ever before. There is a marked increase in the number of young people who disrespect the law, who have little or no regard for the natural rights of others and who apparently have little fear of the consequences of their own deliberate criminal acts. . . . It is hoped that future crimes may be materially lessened by intelligent crime prevention work, but at the present there is no practical substitution for quick, certain and adequate punishment. . . . Burmah White, the penalty I am to impose is not retribution. The law does not wreak vengeance. No amount of punishment can ever wipe out the wrongs you have done or bring back one ray of light in the darkness to the eyes of the unfortunate victim of your criminal enterprise, but it is hoped that your case will serve as an object lesson to others.[1]

In fact, Burmah never spent time at San Quentin but rather was allowed to stay in Los Angeles County Jail until that day in December when she could be brought to the new Tehachapi women's prison in Kern County. The *Herald and Express* discussed Burmah's demeanor in detail, noting that she appeared like a would-be co-ed off for a fashionable weekend:

She babbled gayly about her intention of studying languages at the prison, "majoring" on Russian and German. She declared that she already has a knowledge of French and Spanish.

"I understand," she said, "that the boarders at the women's prison are to have the advantages of bungalow life and education and that such facilities as tennis, volley ball and basketball are to be provided.

I hope there will be movies there, also, although I have heard that there is some question about it although they have them at San Quentin. I intend to make the best of prison life—it will either get me or I will whip it."

Next to the article was an advertisement for *Calling All Cars*, featuring the White case.[2]

The *Herald and Express* played to the popular opinion in the early 1930s that Tehachapi was a "country club." In fact, the prison was so new (Burmah was among the very first inmates) that it was not clear whether it was a proper reformatory that would rehabilitate women in a safe environment—something California clubwomen and other progressives had championed since the early 1900s—or whether it was simply the bars and plaster of San Quentin but in Southern California. Formally known as the California Institution for Women, Tehachapi received a few euphemistic names from its administrators: "campus," "farm," or "reformatory." But in fact, it was a prison—albeit one with very progressive rehabilitation techniques for its time. And there was no tennis court, as Yaw pointed out to the *Bakersfield Californian*.[3]

In her book *Hard Time at Tehachapi: California's First Women's Prison*, Kathleen Cairns writes about the different post-prison experiences of male and female offenders in the early twentieth century. Upon completion of his term, a male offender could change his name, his location, and his occupation. If he knew how to do anything useful, even if it was just unskilled labor, he could find a way to procure food and shelter.[4] A woman, on the other hand, faced a much tougher environment upon her release. "If she has transgressed the social laws—and been caught at it—her fate will be pitiable."[5] Because of this, reformers argued, women offenders needed a facility that could give them job training, hygiene skills, and an education in a safe environment.

For these reformers, the ideal environment would be "a farm, with a calming, healthful, and pastoral environment."[6] And by mid-1934, this is exactly what Tehachapi was, though observers had their doubts early in its history. *LA Times* columnist Harry Carr traveled by buggy with Los Angeles County Sheriff Eugene Biscailuz and some other peace officers to see the institution with his own eyes. His thoughts about it were mixed:

I came back dazed. In buying real estate, I thought I was the world's champion sucker. I yield the palm to the State of California. . . . The new prison lies in a forlorn little valley about five miles out of the town of Tehachapi. The wind howls through there like a tornado. You have to fasten your hat on with adhesive plaster. It is impossible to raise garden vegetables. It is impossible to do anything except hold onto a fence post.[7]

Carr thought the state did a better job hiring an architect for Tehachapi than he did negotiating a good land deal: "The prison buildings are beautiful. It doesn't look like a prison. It is like a resort hotel. The doors are not locked except at night."[8] There was a wire fence and guard towers, but excluding those the vision of Tehachapi was quite lovely. There was an administration building surrounded by four "cottages," residence halls, built with architecture reminiscent of "the French Chateau country": pointed roofs, many windows, trees, lawns and flower gardens with old-fashioned phlox, snapdragons, varicolored sweet peas and hollyhocks.[9] The columnist's final observation was that the "girls" seemed well-behaved and content, thanks to new warden Josephine Jackson, but that boredom was prevalent:

> *In San Quentin, the women were locked up in a house from which they could see a prison filled with men. Too many romantic vibrations. In the new prison, they are bored to tears. Nothing to look at but bare hills. No radios; no place to show talking motion pictures. Nothing to read. Only wind.*[10]

Carr wrote an addendum to his Tehachapi column, noting that he had seen Clara Phillips, who had become "the most influential person in the place—in so far as her effect upon the other women is concerned."[11] Indeed, Burmah had now become part of an "elite" group—a short roster of Tehachapi inmates who remained in the public's consciousness long after their crimes, trials, and incarcerations. Others who had particularly high profiles at that time were Helen Wills Love, Nellie Madison, and Erna Janoschek. Love shot her husband when he refused to take her out with him on New Year's Eve; Madison shot her husband five times, killing him to escape domestic abuse. Janoschek was just seventeen years old when she was convicted of strangling to death a baby she was sitting because it would not stop crying.

But Clara Phillips was Burmah's most notorious prison mate. Dubbed "the Tiger Woman" by the press, Phillips was convicted of beating her husband's alleged paramour to death with a claw hammer in July of 1922. Burmah and Clara were ward mates for about eighteen months before Clara was released in June 1935. Gilbert Brown, columnist for the short-lived *Los Angeles Post-Record*, wrote that with Burmah's arrival, Phillips was no longer the "Problem Child No. 1" at Tehachapi. "Clara Phillips was regarded as a model prisoner," said Brown, "but this Burmah gal is downright ornery. She won't work, and she's mean to everybody."[12]

Brown's probably exaggerated assessment of Burmah's failure to acclimate to life in a reformatory was most certainly a response to a series of columns about Tehachapi that were written by reporter Agness Underwood of the *Los Angeles Herald and Express* in March and April of 1935. Brown was fairly transparent about this when he wrote that although "Blonde Burmah" wrote poetry about "elves and fairies" at "odd moments" at Tehachapi, she was still a burden to the matrons and officials there.[13] Underwood's story about Burmah included the young woman's attempts at prose and her work with the prison newsletter.

The *Herald and Express* reporter's account was, in fact, the only semi-reliable firsthand account of the convicted woman's time in the reformatory, albeit just her first few months. "I interviewed Burmah in jail, during her trial and later in prison," Underwood wrote in her book *Newspaperwoman*. "I didn't talk down to her; nor, despite her youth and new-found notoriety, did I pamper her. I spoke to her reasonably and respectfully—in the sense that I didn't belittle her." Underwood added that Burmah felt like other reporters had done so, and that she chose to speak to Underwood because she seemed to treat her as an "equal." Because of this, alleged the reporter, Burmah freely gave her quotes she would not give anybody else.[14]

Underwood estimated that the Blonde Rattlesnake had shed her scalier skin after sixteen months in prison. "When she entered the institution," she wrote, "Burmah was slightly defiant. Cynical. Egotistical. She had gone through a lot of trouble and had surrounded herself with an atmosphere of 'toughness.'" But on the day she visited in February of 1935, the "blonde bandit girl" was gone. In her place, continued Underwood, there sat a quiet-mannered, sad-eyed girl whose face was framed in soft dark brown hair that she had let grow back to its natural color. "In her place," she repeated, "there is a girl who has given up every plan for the future—whose mind is at present traveling on just one track, and that track says, only "eighteen years, eighteen years, eighteen years."[15]

While Burmah (and Clara and a few others) had more high-profile cases than their reformatory mates who had committed less sensational crimes, they shared statistical similarities with the larger Tehachapi population. Cairns writes that Los Angeles contributed nearly half of all its prisoners and that a full two-thirds came from Southern California. Of the inmates, 80 percent were white, and 90 percent were first-time offenders, like Burmah—though their crimes on the whole were much less violent, mostly crimes against property: grand larceny, forgery, check-kiting, insurance fraud, and other scams. Other crimes included drug offenses, prostitution, bigamy, abortion, even union organizing and vehicle code violations.[16]

Josephine Jackson, who had presided over women prisoners while at San Quentin, was the first warden of Tehachapi. By November 1933, while Burmah was sitting through her trial, Jackson had finished moving all those female inmates into their new Kern County home. "Today," Underwood wrote of the convicts in spring of 1935, "they are settled down to the calm existence of prison life, every day bringing its same thoughts, every day bringing its same tasks, every day bringing its same heartaches through memories."[17] According to Underwood, a convict's day usually went something like this:

Six o'clock is regulation "get up" time—nine o'clock brings "lights out." Work starts immediately after breakfast, when various groups are farmed out for different tasks. Some have chores in the rabbitry, the chicken yard, the barn yard where there are several cows to be milked. And, as groups gather around the electric washing machines, or in the yard planting trees, or in the chicken yard, tending the fowls, loud shouts of laughter may be heard ringing through the echoing mountainous section.

There were no supervisors standing over the inmates, Underwood continued, no one to stand around and scold or correct them. The women were on an honor system to do their best work.[18]

But as Cairns's research shows, administrators carefully controlled all aspects of inmates' lives and labored to control images of prison life given to the public at large by granting access only to reporters who seemed sympathetic to their mission and who were likely to depict their work and the institution environment in positive ways.[19] Underwood was most certainly allowed access to Burmah and the others with the understanding that she would do this. "Recreation is limited at Tehachapi," she wrote, but she noted that each building had a nicely furnished recreation room where the women could gather once their daily tasks were completed. They could play cards, checkers, sew, or play the piano . . . though, because there was no auditorium, the women could not "have any social affairs or even picture shows" because there was no room big enough to seat all of them—though one was built for them a couple of years later. There were even baseball games on Sundays—those who were physically fit enough joined one of two teams who played against each other, and the inmates welcomed the chance to sew their own uniforms.[20]

The healthful qualities of Tehachapi kept Burmah's spirits alive for the first few months of her incarceration. Her "cell" was a front corner room on the second floor of the detention building. Because it was a corner room, it had two windows, both "overlooking the road to freedom," as Underwood dramatically put it. Warden Jackson told Underwood that the inmate was "full of ambition" when she first arrived there and even taught classes in commercial courses, doing "a fine job of it." She taught oral English to other prisoners and typing and dramatics. The widow even started taking University of California extension classes through the mail and started learning how to sew her own blouses. She made basic but cheery curtains to hang around a small mirror on her wall, which she used as an aid when she cut the hair of fellow inmates.

After this initial "settling in," period, however, Burmah received some news that made her realize the bleakness of her situation. On March 20, 1934, the MacKay brothers and George Francis had the unhappy task of telling Burmah that her appeal had been denied in full. Three of the major complaints the trio brought up with regard to her original trial were these:

1. Was the district attorney guilty of misconduct, which denied the appellant a fair and impartial trial?

2. Did the reading of portions of the statement taken before the district attorney before the trial, which listed acts and offenses that Burmah was not ultimately charged with in her indictment, so prejudice the

jury that even the court striking out these statements failed to cure the error?

3. Did the court err in refusing to grant Burmah a continuance when it received proof that her original lawyer (Donald MacKay) was confined to the hospital?

With regard to the first two arguments, appellate judge John M. York acknowledged that the defendant would under ordinary circumstances be entitled to a new trial because alleging that she had participated in crimes for which she was not ultimately charged would be highly prejudicial and unjust. But in this case, he wrote, Burmah's attorneys argued that she thought White "a gentleman" until August 16, when he allegedly forced her to help him steal Leslie Bartel's car and drive it during the shooting of Withington and Allen. Therefore, the jurist continued, it was proper for the prosecution to probe Burmah's memory to see how much she knew about White's crimes *before* August 16, 1933, and to try to ascertain whether she was under duress before that day or whether she was a willing participant.

The problem with this argument put forth by the prosecution (and affirmed by the appellate court) is that Thomas White was not available after September 6 to discuss any crimes he may have committed (with Burmah) before August 16, never mind be charged with them. Essentially, the jury was allowed to hear suppositions of Burmah and Tom's guilt in previous crimes, though neither had been charged with them. For her part, Burmah readily listed all the activities in which she had participated. There was no reason for her to leave any out.

As far as Donald MacKay's illness and inability to represent Burmah, the judge wrote that after examining the entire transcript of the original trial, he found that "she was well and ably represented by counsel throughout the entire proceeding in the trial court." Justice York affirmed all the original court's rulings; there would be no second trial.

It was probably this news that made Burmah get very sick for about two months—the exact illness is not known.[21] Whatever it was, it removed her from her daily distractions and forced her to realize the severity of her penalty. The "gangster's moll" came to the realization, according to Underwood, that she had lost her citizenship and that she was no longer part of the world at large. "I've gone into it very thoroughly," Burmah lamented to Underwood. "The prison board can't do a thing. The judge who sentenced me fixed that, and I just can't see any sense in working hard every day when there's nothing to work for."[22] While she would only be thirty-seven years old upon her release, it must have seemed an eternity to someone who was sentenced at age nineteen. Burmah must have known that her words would be plastered across newspapers everywhere when she confided in Underwood that she was an insomniac, that her brain was "filled with the thoughts of her having 'loved' possibly too well, and always of the heavy price that she is paying, and will continue paying for 16 (more) years and four months, for that sort of 'love.'"[23]

Compounding Burmah's depression was the fact that her father had died while she was in prison. Joseph A. Adams suffered an attack of appendicitis a couple of days after Christmas 1934. He finally went to a Santa Ana hospital to have the infected organ removed on January 7, but he died within hours of the operation's completion. He had little money and no property to leave his family, and thus Mrs. Adams went to work "in the walnuts." She left home at six o'clock in the morning every day and cracked, sorted, and picked out walnut meats for a nearby wholesaler.[24]

In spite of her exhaustion and depression over the loss of her husband, Pearl Adams pleaded with the parole board for her daughter's early release. "Burmah comes from a line of dependable law abiding American families and as far as we have any record, she has not even one ancestor or relative who ever had a criminal charge against them. . . . Burmah was never in trouble of any kind before. . . . She was kind hearted, honest, and always wanted to help us get along, never complaining because I was not able to provide a lot of things that most other girls could have." Adams implored the board interviewer to put in a good report for her daughter, adding that she was just a normal sweet "homeloving" girl, and continued to blame herself for sending her teen out into the world too soon. She lamented that if she had just had enough money to keep Burmah in school a bit longer, she would never have met Tom White. "Any way you wish to look at her case, the fact remains Tom White was entirely responsible for the whole affair. Burmah, beyond a doubt was in his power, either through some influence or through fear and brutal treatment." She maintained that her daughter had been beaten and threatened, but the jury did not get to hear about this. "We do know the latter tactics were used, the prosecution also knew of this evidence but the police prevented it from being brought out at the trial."[25]

Many from the Adamses' community wrote letters or gave interviews in support of Burmah. Nicholas D. Meyer, a friend and neighbor who was also an attorney, wrote favorably on the teen's behalf, as did her Sunday school teacher, Mrs. W. A. Chapman, who called her a "very sweet girl." Mildred Juhnke, who owned the beauty salon where Burmah worked in 1932, made it clear that if the girl had greedy or criminal tendencies, she would have known it. "She was very trustworthy and honest and a good girl, with no bad habits. She stayed at my home at times also. So I feel I really know her. She had full charge of this place of business and there was never a missing penny."[26] Ten persons from Burmah's neighborhood signed a petition urging an early release for her.

As would be expected, the LAPD and District Attorney's Office did not support early release for the woman they helped to convict. "This party drove the car," says a typed missive from a spokesman from law enforcement, dated July 21, 1934. "White used a revolver. . . . This party stood or sat in car during robberies, laughing or smiling, and in such ways showed a hardened and cold-blooded disposition."[27]

In May 1937 a new warden replaced Jackson, and this new regime helped Burmah keep her spirits up, in spite of the parole board's repeated denials of release for her.[28] Florence Monahan was a longtime reformer, having spent many years implementing changes at Minnesota's Shakopee Reformatory and as an advocate for women in court. Monahan argued that prisons ought to have conditions that will produce "self-respecting citizens" instead of "bitter, beaten" women who leave prison determined to "get back" at society.[29] Monahan did away with uniforms and allowed Burmah and her fellow inmates to create their own, season-appropriate frocks, albeit within certain shape and color parameters. Each woman was allowed to choose her own material and style that she felt suited her best, subject to Monahan's approval. The warden also allowed the women to adorn their rooms, celebrate holidays with decorations of their own choosing and making, and wear jewelry and cosmetics.

Monahan also promoted activities that supported physical and mental health. She put the prisoners on a merit system, with time off sentences for good behavior. To be sure, the usual work periods remained, but women could choose to spend some of their labor time learning a trade, like assisting a dentist, cosmetology (Burmah was allowed to teach courses in the subject), waitressing, and sewing. Some of the most coveted positions within Tehachapi were those of writer or editor for the *Clarion*, and Burmah garnered two such positions: associate editor and reporter.

Started in April 1937, the *Clarion* was the only prison publication in the country printed on an institution's premises. Tehachapi trustee Lotus Loudon donated printing equipment from his own plant at the Anaheim *Bulletin*, which he founded in 1923. The female inmates built the pressroom themselves, remodeling a "noxious, barn-like" building that had once housed rabbits.[30] Because the stories were of course censored by prison officials, it could be easy to dismiss them as unrepresentative of what life was really like for the inmates at Tehachapi, but the stories should not be dismissed, argues Kathleen Cairns. Certainly, only those women who were articulate, creative, talented, and deemed suitable for rehabilitation were considered for jobs on the *Clarion*, but the content gave lie to the common perception that inmates were "coarse, common and uneducated."[31]

For the *Clarion*'s inaugural issue, Burmah wrote a story called "Parole." The story and the edition itself are not extant but were most certainly influenced either factually or emotionally, or both, by the experiences of her two parole applications thus far, one in 1935 and one in 1936, both of which were denied without comment.[32] The *Santa Ana Register* liked to keep abreast of what their famous inmate was doing to pass the time in prison, and it printed an article about Burmah's poetry that was sent to San Quentin to be printed in its *Bulletin* newsletter before Tehachapi founded the *Clarion*. Although she was sentenced to a possible life term, reported the *Register*, "Burmah White is still alive" and writing "verse that came from a cell in a wall-less women's prison" in Tehachapi:

The Brownie, the Fairy and You

I looked and saw a fairy perched
upon
Your shoulder, beckoning to me.
Entranced,
All motion from my body fled. A
fawn
Might then have passed by, unafraid
or danced
On cool dew–covered lawn ten tiny
elves;
Such was the silence that engulfed us both.
Again the fairy waved to moonlit
shelves,
Raised high a tiny hand in fairy
oath
Proclaiming beauty wild,
and sweet, and rare,
Alluring me to join the revelry.
Yet still I lingered, hesitant to
bare
My weeping heart for glancing
sword to see.
A jovial little brownie tiptoed to
my side and whispered:
"Walk with her—forgive.
"It is true that only the fearless
live."[33]

Burmah also wrote recipes for the prison's cookbook and took classes to become certified in medical billing and general office management. Her closest friend and confidant for many years was Florence Inman, who was serving a sentence for forging checks.[34]

Burmah White applied for parole five times between 1935 and 1939; the State Board of Prison Terms and Paroles denied her all five times. Florence Monahan wrote terse statements about each prisoner who applied for parole. In November 1938 the warden noted of Burmah, "This inmate worked well. Attitude not the best, but has been spoiled by too much attention, especially from former physician: now improving in general attitude," and in November 1939, "General conduct and attitude very much improved. . . . Has had two reports for disobedience and insolence since last appearance."[35]

As was customary, the secretary of the Board of Trustees of the California Institution for Women sought statements from the victims about what it would mean to them to either grant parole or withhold it. Emily D. Latham attempted to interview the most aggrieved victim, Cora Withington, but was summarily blocked by Harold "Hal" Ashley, a lawyer for Standard Oil Company, and his wife, clubwoman Annie Ashley. Hal Ashley, who was treasurer of the fund raised by the parents of many of Miss Withington's pupils to care for her after her misfortune, was adamantly opposed to such an interview and telegrammed Secretary Latham:

Regarding attitude of group which sponsored Withington fund toward consideration by your board at this time of White parole application: opinion is adverse unanimously. Board should bear in mind between six and seven thousand contributors to fund and certainty of strong adverse publicity in Southern California newspapers all of which gave unlimited support to fund movement. Mrs. Walter Van Dyke feels that proper training for parole could not have been received under conditions prevailing prior to recent reorganization of prison administration.[36]

Mrs. Walter Van Dyke was also a clubwoman and a member of the board at Children's Hospital Los Angeles. Husband Walter was, like Hal Ashley, an investment banker and attorney, as were the husbands of many other women involved with the Withington fund. Latham acquiesced to the wishes of these fund managers and their wives, and Cora was never interviewed.

In November 1939 Superintendent Monahan provided a pre-parole report to the Board of Prisons. In it she noted that Burmah desired parole and that the institution had received word from a San Francisco dentist that he would provide employment for her should she be released. Dr. Louis Lichtenstein had been her dentist when she had lived in the Bay Area before the earthquake in 1933, and he thought her medical assistant training in Tehachapi could be of use to his office. Some of his closest friends, noted Lichtenstein, were notable police chiefs and senators from the San Francisco area. In other words, he had every confidence that Burmah was of no further threat to society.

The Los Angeles district attorney and Judge Bowron felt differently. The former opposed parole or further leniency "because of the character of the offense of which defendant was convicted." Bowron's negative statement toward parole, dated June 25, 1937, accompanied all of Burmah's subsequent parole applications: "By reason of the number and nature of the serious crimes of which this woman stands convicted, I assume that the Board is not contemplating a parole for a long period of time. If the Members of the Board are not fully advised as to the facts and if the facts do not sufficiently appear from the record now before you, I would be glad to supply additional information if the application for parole is to be at all seriously considered."[37] Once again, on November 18, 1939, the board denied Burmah parole. It met again on April 19, 1940, and was given an updated statement from Warden Monahan regarding the infamous inmate: "Has had a perfect record since last appearance November 1939. Works well, cooperates, is pleasant and agreeable." These words did not make a difference in any future parole requests because, at this time, Burmah decided she would serve her full term. "Thinks that is the wisest thing to do since her sentence expires in December 1943," reported Monahan. "Dreads the newspaper howl if she were paroled."[38]

CHAPTER 9

The Malignancy of This Thing

BURMAH'S RELEASE FROM TEHACHAPI ON DECEMBER 1, 1941, WENT largely unnoticed by press syndicates. By the time they picked up on this item, the world was already engrossed with Japan's bombing of Pearl Harbor and America's entry into World War II.

She was not on parole but rather released from custody with no further obligations. The *Los Angeles Times* and other papers asked Mary B. King of Santa Monica, chairman of the Board of Trustees for the California Institution for Women at Tehachapi, why Burmah had been released when her term was fixed at twelve and a half years. King replied that White had earned time off her sentence for good behavior. The board may also have taken mercy on Burmah, as the *Evening Herald and Express* mentioned that she had undergone several operations that last year, including one for a thyroid disorder "which almost caused her death."[1] In all likelihood, Burmah was sent away as most inmates from Tehachapi were: with twenty dollars, a set of new clothes, and a hug from fellow prisoners for good luck.[2]

Burmah White was at odds about where to start over after her release. While she was happy not to have to check in with a parole officer every month or so, she was—in fact—rudderless. She returned to her family's home in Santa Ana, which was comforting if not depressing because of her father's absence. Burmah knew she would be a burden—she had been out of the job market for eight years, and her mother could barely cover her own expenses and those of Jo Louraine. She missed her mother and sister desperately, but she could see that if she returned to Santa Ana permanently, she would subject Jo Louraine, who was now in high school and thriving, to all her notoriety and gossip. By the end of January 1942, the "Blonde Rattlesnake" was already ensconced in San Francisco. She enrolled in California Secretarial School and graduated at the top of her class.

It was probably Burmah's former employer, dentist Louis Lichtenstein, who introduced Burmah to Edmond E. Herrscher, who at the time of her employment was a divorce attorney. He was also embroiled in his own legal and family matters: Before he married her, socialite Fannie May Howard Herrscher was married to Charles S. Howard, an automobile tycoon, famous for owning Seabiscuit, the unlikely champion Thoroughbred that captured American hearts in the 1930s. When Fannie May died in 1942, Herrscher and her sons with Howard clashed over her estate.

Herrscher abandoned his law practice and invested in high-end grocery store chains in the Bay Area, including Eezy-Freezy Food Stores (he would later run Mayfair Markets), and other large corporations. Later, in the late 1950s, Herrscher made headlines for developing Century City, a 175-acre upscale business district adjacent to the Twentieth Century Fox film studio lot. While Herrscher's papers don't specifically refer to Burmah White, they do reveal that he was a man captivated by beautiful women and notoriety—he frequently dined with starlets and the wives or mistresses of actors and other businessmen.[3] He fancied himself a movie script writer and married four times—three times to very wealthy women.

Herrscher hired Burmah to supervise management, purchasing, development, and sales of various properties. She worked closely with CPAs and attorneys, and handled various financial aspects of some transactions. The fact that the press did not harass Burmah in San Francisco may well have been due to the fact that Herrscher kept very tight security at his offices and that his legal team consistently kept reporters away from him and his family. This worked well—until Herrscher took valuable paintings, furniture, cash, and jewelry from his dead wife's separate property that belonged to her sons. Herrscher's stepsons had to get police and a locksmith involved to be able to serve a court summons to him at his office. From then on the press fairly camped out on his office and home doorsteps for the next few years as the case wound through the courts and a subsequent marriage produced a similar, hotly contested divorce settlement.[4]

One night in 1945 or 1946, Burmah met a client of Herrscher's. Alfred Gray Dymond was ten years older than Burmah and married to his second wife, with whom he had three children. Dymond was a gifted structural engineer and often hired to consult for large municipal projects. They started a romantic affair, and Dymond rented a new house for her in Walnut Creek, a suburb east of San Francisco.

In the wee hours of the morning of Wednesday, October 26, 1949, Burmah drove her convertible down a main thoroughfare in Walnut Creek, apparently on her way home from somewhere. She was driving at sixty-five or seventy miles an hour, according to police, when she hit a railroad crossing signal at the Sacramento Northern crossing on Main Street. Her vehicle careened north, smashed a detour barricade and side-swiped a parked sedan. The convertible then went through a small fence and scattered a pile of sewer pipe stacked alongside the road. Still, Burmah's car continued, hit a bus, and shoved the vehicle twenty feet before finally coming to a stop.

Burmah was taken to the hospital, and amazingly she only had a cut lip. Afterward, she was arrested for drunk driving but released within hours on her own recognizance because the crimes were then considered misdemeanors. She was fined $250 and paid the estimated $3,000 damages, and there was no further punishment.[5] Burmah continued to work for Herrscher until the end of 1950. On January 27, 1951, the former Mrs. White and Dymond got married in Reno, Nevada, with only Jo Louraine and a friend of Dymond's in attendance.

By the mid-1950s Dymond had had enough of the San Francisco Bay Area. It was expensive, his ex-wife Edith was always afoot, and he had been sued for failure to pay a subcontractor on a project south of the city. His mentor and the owner of the construction conglomerate for which he worked had been killed when his truck crashed into a Southern Pacific freight train at a crossing, and Dymond did not get along with the succeeding managers. He and Burmah moved to Seattle, where an apartment development contract awaited him.

Ellery Esau Cuff became a deputy county public defender two years after the doors closed behind Burmah Adams White in Tehachapi. Cuff's first cases as defender were unique. His first was *California v. Leroy Drake* in late 1935, in which Drake—nineteen years old—killed his aunt and uncle by putting poison in their coffee, stuffed them in their car, and then shoved the vehicle off a cliff, taking their bodies with it to the bottom of the Los Angeles Harbor. With less than twenty-four hours to prepare for Drake's defense when the latter's private attorney quit, Cuff successfully argued insanity, garnering the teen a life sentence at San Quentin instead of the death penalty. In the months following, Cuff defended accused wife killers (including one who did it with rattlesnakes), alleged mob assassins, and child murderers.

Born to a poor farmer in Trinity County, California, in 1896, Cuff left home at fourteen to work at a gold dredging plant on the Yuba River. He did this kind of physical labor for ten long years, moving from one mine to another, from one public works project to the next up and down the eastern Sierras of California. Cuff was drafted for WWI in 1918 and, because he had a background in telegraphy, was sent to New York for additional training. While there, he and all his bunkmates got the influenza that was ravaging the world. One by one his dozen or so dorm friends died and were carted off. Cuff was the only survivor of that class of would-be soldiers, and the army sent him back home after several months of recuperation. He attributed his survival to having been lucky enough to have the only bed next to a window, which let in fresh air.[6]

Cuff decided to study law, something he'd thought about since he was a child. He attended college at St. Mary's in Moraga, California, and earned a spot in USC's law school graduating class of 1924. He paid for both degrees with the currency he earned working his mine-related jobs up north: gold dust. Cuff accepted a job with Los Angeles County's probation department then transferred to the public defender's office in 1928.

That office had been established only fourteen years earlier, in 1913, and was the first of its kind in the nation.[7] It started with just one attorney and one stenographer and was still composed of only five attorneys by the time of Burmah White's trial in 1933. It was not a perfect system, but it was looked upon as a good example by other major cities in the country, and Cuff's boss was often quoted in newspaper articles about offering free legal aid to indigent citizens: "It is as much the function of the State to protect innocent persons as it is to send guilty persons to punishment. It is not a matter of charity. The State having brought the defendant to trial should itself protect the accused to the extent of securing and insuring a fair trial."[8] Cuff cleaved to this idea wholeheartedly. "The only reason for our office," Cuff once told an employee, "is to help people in trouble."[9]

He might have wound up as Burmah White's public defender were it not for a young man named Leo Dwight Murphy, dubbed by newspapers as the "Long Beach Wife Killer." Seven years before, in 1926, Murphy had beaten his bride of three weeks so savagely that she died a few days later. He fled Los Angeles, crisscrossing the country to avoid capture, taking a new bride along the way. But on July 7, 1933, detectives caught up with him in Pittsburgh and brought him back to Southern California to face trial, which commenced two weeks later. It isn't clear how Cuff defended Murphy, but it did not work: Murphy was found guilty of first-degree murder and torture. The young defense attorney immediately filed an appeal, arguing that Murphy was "not capable mentally of forming a deliberate and premeditated attempt to kill," owing to his extreme alcoholism—evidence showed that the Long Beach man drank bitters that were up to 50 percent alcohol in content.[10] The Supreme Court denied Cuff's appeal, and Murphy was sent to San Quentin to await his execution date. Cuff spent the next year filing briefs to the governor of California, asking him to commute the killer's sentence to life in prison instead. This also failed, and Murphy was hanged on December 7, 1934.

Murphy's case weighed especially hard on Cuff, and the defense lawyer redoubled his efforts to make the courts consider a defendant's circumstances, such as income, intelligence, abuse, or addiction. By the time Burmah White appeared at his office in August 1954, Cuff was head of the public defender's office. He managed a staff of twenty deputies and shepherded about six thousand cases per year. At this stage in his career, he was far too "upper management" to handle a mere pardon case for a forty-one-year-old housewife who had been convicted twenty-one years earlier. These non-trial, nonurgent things were best handled by lower-level employees. But Cuff was intrigued by Burmah's case, and after receiving a letter from her asking for help, he agreed to meet with her.

Burmah told Cuff her entire version of the events that had put her in jail, and why she was now seeking a pardon. He put a summary of this saga on her application for clemency:

The reasons for this application after twenty-two long and difficult years are many: to further protest my innocence I must do, but the primary purpose in taking this action is to gain those civil rights of a decent citizen. The malignancy of this thing has been such as to seriously undermine both my physical and neural health. Now, my marital life may be jeopardized in that my husband's business may take him abroad. Naturally, I should like to accompany him.[11]

Cuff gave a lot of thought to Burmah's ordeal. Obtaining executive clemency was not an easy task, especially if the felon resided in another state. It was entirely the governor's decision whether to grant this forgiveness, and the governor did not hand these orders out freely. A pardon was an act of grace and forgiveness, not an acknowledgment that justice was not served or that a prison sentence was unjust. The act partially or totally relieved the pardoned individual from some of the ramifications of the original sentence. In most states, at the time of Burmah's application in 1955, a person could apply for a pardon after being convicted of a crime and after having exhausted his or her judicial appeals. Pardons could also be granted to people who were no longer incarcerated but who wished to regain certain rights that were lost or suspended on conviction, such as the right to vote, testify, serve on a jury, hold public office, or practice a profession.

The governor, in turn, relied on the recommendation of Adult Authority, an office within the Department of Corrections. The Adult Authority subscribed to the basic philosophy that all segments of the field of criminal justice should coordinate their efforts to attain a primary purpose: the protection of society. The entity further subscribed to the philosophy that society is best protected by preserving human values to the maximum extent possible, including those of the felon, through restoring him so he can regain his rightful place in the social order as early as possible.

A pardon could also restore the right to travel overseas, which is the main reason Burmah wished to obtain one, given Alfred's travels across the Canadian and Mexican borders for business. In fact, Burmah was really trying to hold on to her marriage. Months before her application for a pardon, she filed for divorce against Dymond, citing "cruelty," the usual "box-check" at that time for a couple who is fighting a lot. It could not have been lost on Burmah that she met Alfred at a time when he was traveling quite a bit and still married to his previous wife.[12]

To start, Cuff advised, Burmah would need to fill out and file forms with the governor's office, signaling that she was formally applying for clemency. She was required to post her goal for four weeks in a newspaper in the county in which she was convicted, so she took an advertisement in the *Los Angeles Daily Journal*: "Please take notice, that I, Burmah A. Dymond (formerly Burmah A. White), convicted of the crimes of 1st degree robbery, attempted robbery . . . will apply to His Excellency, Goodwin J. Knight, Governor of the State of California, for a pardon."[13] The former "gangster moll" made another trip to California in February 1955 and from her mother's house in Santa Ana formally applied for clemency.

Burmah's first letters were probably the hardest for her to write. She was required by the State of California to get letters of recommendation from the attorneys who had prosecuted her in the first place, and so she asked George Stahlman and Grant Cooper for letters of support. Cooper's arrived at Governor Knight's office first, dated February 28, 1955. It read, in part:

> *Since she was only nineteen years of age at the time this offense was committed, and, generally speaking, under the domination of a man with whom she was keeping company who was primarily guilty and was killed at the time of her arrest, I have no hesitancy in recommending that she be given a pardon for the purpose of restoring her civil rights. Mr. Cuff has informed me that she is married, living in Seattle, and has lived an exemplary life since her release in 1941.*

Stahlman's handwritten letter arrived at Governor Knight's office about a month later. After a summary of Burmah's case, he wrote:

My recollection is that she was about 18 or 19 years old at the time of her offences and madly in love with White.

After her conviction and sentence I visited her in the county jail. Her attitude was one of grief, sorry and understanding of her errors.

Several years later on a visit to Tehachapi I talked with her and was convinced that she had cooperated in every way to rehabilitate herself.

I know nothing of her conduct since release from prison.

If she has conducted herself since that time in a law abiding and proper manner I would have no hesitancy in recommending her pardon.[14]

Burmah's former employers, Herrscher and Robinson, and friend Louis Lichtenstein also wrote glowing recommendations, discussing her ability to run an office with intelligence and integrity. Cuff suggested Burmah give a reason she quit working, since she was well regarded in the professional capacity: "Nervous exhaustion was the cause of my leaving the active business world," she wrote.[15] The Adult Authority office also received a number of endorsements from friends and family of the Adamses.

A few weeks before Thanksgiving in 1956, Adult Authority met in San Francisco to consider all the facets of Burmah's application for clemency. Four days later, Chairman E. W. Lester typed his final recommendation to Governor Knight:

On that date [November 1, 1956] Adult Authority recommended subject's application for <u>pardon to be granted</u>. The Adult Authority believes that this recommendation to be justified on the grounds of complete rehabilitation, evidenced by fifteen years of good conduct and social adjustment. Applicant has been active in civic affairs and is happily married to a successful business man who has been an exceedingly good influence on her. Applicant was only 19 years old at the *time she committed the offenses in question, and while there can be no excuse for her participation therein, there is no doubt but that she was dominated by her first husband, an older man with a prior prison record. Particular attention is called to the fine report received from the parole authorities in the State of Washington, where the applicant is presently residing, indicating that she would be a credit to any community. Of further interest is the applicant's desire to become active in the Orthopedic Hospital in Seattle.*[16]

Ruth Huggett, a parole officer with the State of Washington's Board of Prison Terms and Paroles, wrote in favor of pardoning Burmah.

Thad "Frank" Brown, chief of detectives for the LAPD in 1955 and chief of the whole department ten years later, disagreed. He wrote Governor Knight's office with an official opinion from the LAPD:

A review of the circumstances surrounding her convictions has been made by this office and owing to the cold bloodedness and lack of feeling toward others in the commission of these crimes, it is our recommendation that no consideration be extended this petitioner in her application for a certificate of rehabilitation and pardon.[17]

As well, there was a letter from David Coleman, a Los Angeles Superior Court judge. The Adult Authority, as a matter of course, would send a form letter to a presiding judge in the court where the felon was convicted. Coleman wrote that, although he had no knowledge of the case, he read the transcript with Fletcher Bowron's words on it: "the heartless and wanton shooting of Cora B. Withington and Crombie Allen." Additionally, he noted, the record showed that the defendant participated in more armed holdups after the maiming of Withington and Allen. For this reason, he could not make a favorable recommendation for granting a pardon to Burmah White.[18] For nearly a year and a half, Burmah heard nothing, and then in December 1957, she got news she had been dreading: "Dear Mrs. Dymond," said a typewritten letter, "This is to advise you that Governor Knight has considered your application for a pardon and has concluded from the record that no grounds exist which would warrant the granting of executive clemency." Knight gave no further details.[19]

Over the next few years, Burmah and Alfred Dymond led a comfortable if isolated existence in Seattle. Dymond's children had long stopped speaking to him, owing to his desertion of their mother and his hard drinking. The couple rented a house in Seattle's fashionable Magnolia district until 1960, when they were able to move into an apartment in a luxury building he helped build in the wealthy Capitol Hill neighborhood. They did not have many friends, and since their building catered to wealthy retirees, there were not very many people Burmah felt comfortable socializing with as neighbors. Dymond worked long hours and traveled to Mexico and Canada for work for long periods of time.

Burmah's mother, Pearl Adams, passed away in Santa Ana on June 25, 1962, at the age of seventy-two; for whatever reason, Burmah could not make it to her funeral. Jo Louraine and her second husband scraped together enough money to buy a plot for Pearl at the local cemetery where her husband, Joseph, was laid to rest.

While there is often no one reason for someone to drink alcoholically, it may have been the news of her mother's death, her isolation, or simply her predisposition to drink that spurred Burmah to drink heavily.[20] On a fall day in 1962, Alfred Dymond came home from work and discovered his wife on the floor, dead. Because of her young age, the medical examiner performed an autopsy. Burmah Adams White Dymond died of "acute cerebral edema"—swelling of the brain—due to "acute alcoholism." The coroner noted that her blood alcohol level was "in excess of .30 mg%." She passed away on September 6—the same day that, twenty-nine years earlier, husband Tom White had been killed.[21]

Burmah was cremated and then reinterred with her mother and father in Orange County, California. Alfred Dymond died just months after his wife, on December 8, 1962, also of acute alcoholism.[22]

CHAPTER 10

Vanished from Public View

ON NOVEMBER 16, 1933, EXACTLY ONE WEEK AFTER BURMAH ARLINE Adams White was sentenced to spend thirty years of her life in prison, a Los Angeles jury acquitted a man named William A. Freericks on charges of impersonating a federal officer.

A report provided to then–FBI chief J. Edgar Hoover summarizes the incidents that got Freericks arrested. On March 25, 1933, four men went to the residence of a couple named Turbyfill in Los Angeles. Freericks, using the alias William Dawson, stated that he was a federal Prohibition officer and that he had a search warrant for their premises. While "Dawson" was talking to the couple, showing fake federal documents, three other men in official-looking jackets went around back to search the garage. It is not clear whether they found booze or just knew that Turbyfill sometimes sold it from his home, but it was abundantly clear that Freericks told the couple that $150 could "clear everything" and there would be no arrests. The liquor-selling couple decided they would rather take their chances in court than part with $150, so they told an agent they knew to be real. Freericks was arrested the next day when an officer pretending to be a delivery boy brought what the con thought was cash.

While under interrogation for this crime, Freericks admitted to hijacking liquor from November 1932 to about April 1933 and using fake Prohibition agent badges on many of those occasions. He preyed chiefly on bootleggers but also was suspected of being involved with the murder of a gangster known as Robert John Busey, who was a chief competitor in the booze smuggling business.

Federal agents could not make the Turbyfill or the Busey crimes stick to Freericks. The witnesses to both transgressions could not identify his accomplices, and the radio salesman–turned-thug would not admit to any involvement in either. He did, however, concede that he might have had some part in robbing Mrs. Fred Cullen of South Orange Drive in Los Angeles on May 10, 1933. In this instance, he and two accomplices went to her home, showed their bogus badges and search warrants, and located three pints of whiskey in the house. The men demanded a settlement from Cullen—diamonds or furs would suffice if she did not have any cash. Finally, Cullen agreed to pay one hundred dollars drawn on her bank and later showed this cashed check receipt to the LAPD as proof of Freericks's deception. He was arrested then but bonded out and skipped his court appearance. The robbery detail detective who intercepted the Freericks-Cullen case was Harry R. Maxwell.

Whatever Maxwell and his colleagues found in Burmah and Tom White's residence on September 6, 1933—including at least Laura Freericks's driver's license in Burmah's bag—was enough for the lieutenant to apprehend Freericks, which he did on September 7. He placed the criminal in Lincoln Heights City Jail to await grand jury consideration of his charges of extortion. In contrast, the FBI's report on Freericks says that it was their interception of mail to his mother and sister in Arizona that led to their knowledge of his address and therefore his arrest. In other words, both agencies took credit for his capture.

The connection between Tom and Burmah White and the Freerickses is murky. It is entirely possible the two couples were merely social friends, brought together by simply being young and childless in Los Angeles, and enjoying the "big city scene." Perhaps the items belonging to the Freerickses were there because they had enjoyed some food and drinks in an apartment building where they might have had mutual acquaintances. Maybe the Whites were robbing the robbers, or vice versa. But this, in addition to the fact that the other men arrested at the apartment building had done some "jobs" with William Freericks, suggests that the couples at least knew each other more than in passing. Indeed, Burmah and the young Laura Freericks would have had a lot in common: They were just a few years apart in age; they were both beauty salon employees, possibly at the same business on Wilshire Boulevard; and they were both second wives to felonious men. William Freericks and Laura Powell married August 5, 1933, using the same courthouse and judge in Santa Ana that Tom White and Burmah Adams used some twenty-five days later.

For robbery detective Harry Maxwell, it may have been dumb luck that he found the Freerickses' current residential information in the Whites' apartments. Whatever the case, the Freericks situation was peeled away from the Burmah White case, and they never met again. Maxwell did not even participate in Burmah's trial, owing to his work on this other case. Ultimately, Freericks was acquitted of extorting Mrs. Cullen. But the Volstead Act was repealed in December of 1933, effectively ending Prohibition, and there was no reason for the FBI to continue using resources to link together the Freerickses' crimes that might have represented a larger federal conspiracy. This all means that Maxwell either spared Burmah the association with even more serious, federal crimes or used the Freerickses' items in her building as a pretext for involving himself in the federal case.

The Freerickses were not the only arrests made on evidence found at the Whites' apartment building the day of Tom's death and Burmah's arrest—just the highest profile one. On November 1, 1933—two days before the official end of the Blonde Rattlesnake's trial—the *LA Times* reported that five more criminal suspects had been "ferreted out of their places of seclusion," thanks to a "clew" found when Thomas White was slain:

Investigating officers reported they have definite information linking the suspects with the $4850 bank messenger robbery May 13, last, in Long Beach. At that time two messengers of the Security-First National bank were held up by a trio of gunmen. The officers also say they are conducting an investigation in an effort to have the suspects identified as the bandits who robbed the Van Nuys branch of the Bank of America and a Vermont-avenue branch of the same bank. . . . At the time White was killed in a shooting affray with police in his Third-street district apartment-house, the officers says, they obtained information that pointed to [Melvin N.] Johnson and the four other suspects.[1]

Tom White may have confronted LAPD officers with a gun on that fateful day of September 6 knowing that he would never see the light of day again if he were arrested—not just for the Withington-Allen shooting but also because of his possible part in robbing banks and a ring that impersonated federal officers.

On September 8, 1933, San Marino housewife Mrs. Edwin M. Porter wrote to detectives Anderson, Bergeron, Burris, and Maxwell:

> *I cannot refrain from writing to express to you my appreciation of your wonderful courage in capturing the desperate criminal White and his accomplice. . . . I moved to this community last February from a small town in Indiana. Naturally there would be more crime in a large city, and also it would be so very much harder to trace them, the criminals, so I am overwhelmed at the audacity of the bandits and criminals of all kinds.*
>
> *My dear sirs, I hope you will accept my poor effort at commendation for your bravery, in the spirit in which I send it. It is very sincere, and I would like to see you and all officers of the law who risk their lives to make safe the lives of the people, given a huge parade demonstration or any big evidence of the people's appreciation. If the governors would do their part and quit paroling criminals, it would make it less difficult for the officers, and the tax payers.*[2]

Indeed, Burmah's arrest and trial spurred a lot of newspaper ink about California's "secret parole" system, which refers to the state's "indeterminate sentence" law passed seventeen years prior. Simply speaking, the goal of this law was to relieve overcrowding in prisons, and to give reformed criminals a chance to reintroduce themselves to normal society. The *Herald and Express* wrote that as a result of Tom White's shooting of Withington, a petition was circulating that as of November 4, 1933, already had more than three thousand signatures. It was disturbing, it said, that a parole system could turn a hardened criminal loose without adequate public safeguard. "Secret parole hearings," continued the article, "are just as obnoxious to spirit of the American people. Parole hearings should be announced in advance and made as public as the usual court procedure."[3]

Judge Fletcher Bowron took up the "no secret parole" cause as a result of Burmah's trial. At the very least, the jurist told various law and citizen groups over the next couple of years, there should be a partial remedy: The trial judge should be allowed to fix the minimum term of imprisonment, and parole should only be granted after a public hearing.[4] By the beginning of 1935, Bowron had largely moved on from this issue. It had been co-opted by Buron Fitts, Chief Davis, and a lieutenant of J. Edgar Hoover, who suggested that all law enforcement organizations of the nation be coordinated like the military, as "one great army to move against crime."[5]

In 1938 Bowron won a recall election against Mayor Shaw. For fifteen years he was continually reelected to this important position—fifteen years of tremendous growth and unusual problems for the Los Angeles area, mainly relations with Mexican, African-American, and Japanese immigrants and citizens in the region during and after World War II. Following Japan's attack on Pearl Harbor on December 7, 1941, Bowron reassured listeners on his weekly radio program that there was no threat of an attack on Southern California shores. However, by January 1942, Bowron became one of the early elected officials to call for the incarceration of Japanese Americans, urging that Japanese Americans be moved several miles inland and be put to work raising food and performing other jobs for the war effort. In spite of this complicated piece of history, Bowron was credited as being the major force in cleaning up the city government of links to racketeering, graft, prostitution, and gambling.[6] He passed away in 1968.

Bowron's place in history will always be intertwined with that of Buron Fitts, Frank Shaw, and James "Two Gun" Davis. The "Shaw spoils system" went into effect in July 1933, when Shaw was elected mayor: City contracts were awarded without competitive bidding, people in city government were paid to use designated contractors, and large industries were solicited for bribes in return for the Shaw administration's sponsoring of legislation designed to drive their smaller competitors out of business. Meanwhile, Frank's brother Joe was selling LAPD jobs, the answer keys to exams, and hard-to-get Depression-era promotions, right out of his City Hall office. Simultaneously, the LAPD's Central Vice Squad roamed the city, serving as the ultimate enforcer and collector of organized vice

operations, with the take going all the way up the line to the central orga-
nizer, Joe Shaw.[7]

It took the "square-jawed courage" of Bowron, former LAPD detective–turned-private-eye Harry Raymond, and former missionary-turned–
restaurant mogul Clifford Clinton to expose the corruption triangle of
the Shaws, Fitts, and Davis. The police department's intelligence squad
was so desperate to shut them up that it blew up Raymond's car, nearly
killing him. It was this bombing that made the public so outraged that it
voted Shaw out of office, one of the first recalls of a big-city mayor in US
history, and forced Davis and twenty-three other high-ranking LAPD
officers to submit resignations.[8]

After Davis resigned, he worked at Douglas Aircraft Company in
Santa Monica as head of plant protection but resigned a few years later
due to ill health. He died from a stroke in June 1949 while on vacation in
Montana. Fitts survived an assassination attempt in 1937; he recovered
completely and remained in office until 1940, when he was defeated by
reform candidate John F. Dockweiler. Fitts retired to Three Rivers, Tulare
County, California. He committed suicide on March 29, 1973. He was
seventy-eight years old.

Robert G. "Bob" Wheeler, confined mostly to procedural matters
during the Burmah White trial, left his private practice in 1941 when
Buron Fitts's successor appointed him deputy district attorney. Wheeler
was one of the lead attorneys assigned by District Attorney Dockweiler
to look into the death of Stanley Beebe. Beebe, taken into custody in
December 1942 on a public intoxication charge, was released a day later,
complaining of stomach pain from a savage beating he'd received from
officers. Ten days after returning home, he died, according to the coroner,
as a result of a violent external blow. Over the course of the next year,
LAPD officers gave statements that they had seen colleagues beat Beebe
but then recanted as part of a larger cover-up of police brutality by the
police commission. Inexplicably, during the trial of the alleged murderer,
Officer Compton P. Dixon, in June 1943, Wheeler pointed the finger at
Beebe's widow, telling the courtroom that she should be investigated for
the killing of her husband. Wheeler may have fallen prey to the strong-
arm tactics of Dixon's defense attorney, Samuel F. Rummel, known as

the "mouthpiece" for gangster Mickey Cohen and other "underworld" figures.[9]

In 1955 the Wheelers were clearing brush from a lot they owned in Malibu when Mrs. Wheeler turned around and realized that her husband was no longer there. A friend who had been helping them found Wheeler dead on the beach two hundred feet below. His widow told reporters that he had suffered from a heart condition for some time.[10]

The year after Burmah's trial, Olin MacKay—her "accidental" lawyer—ran for a superior court judgeship. He did not win. Additionally, in August 1934 he was sanctioned by Buron Fitts for failure to show on time in court while acting as sole counsel for criminal defendants. He and a partner were disbarred in 1937 for employing a known felon to perform legal duties in their office and pretend he was an attorney in court—MacKay never gave a reason publicly for hiring this person. For a few years, MacKay made a living as a ship parts salesman; strangely, shortly after the end of World War II, he was able to get his license to practice law reinstated. MacKay passed away in 1954.

George Haywood Francis, who fought tooth and nail for Burmah, spent a couple of years after the trial working for the City of Los Angeles, defending clients facing the most serious of charges, such as murder and felony assault. Around 1935 he went back into private practice and again found himself squaring off against City Attorney Cooper, who, in turn, was fending off inquiries into a wiretap found in the office of City Councilman Stephen Cunningham. It was not very difficult for Cunningham's secretary to figure out her boss's office was bugged, owing to the sudden rental of the office space next door and the peculiar attention paid to the suite by a window washer who did not seem to get dirty. When she and her colleagues discovered the device, the police and Mayor Bowron immediately got involved, as did Francis, who was then personal counsel to Cunningham. On May 5, 1941, Cooper gave a statement to the police and reporters that he thought someone planted the device with the intention of having it discovered so that this person or persons could cast blame on Mayor Bowron and make him look bad in his bid for another term as mayor—the other candidate being Councilman Cunningham. Francis fired back immediately, in the *Times*:

Grant Cooper is the son-in-law of Mayor Bowron's personal secretary. I am advised that he has said he obtained affidavits from parties purporting to have participated in or had knowledge of installation of the recording equipment on Friday, the day before any official of the Cunningham campaign suspected the presence of the dictograph.

This confirms my suspicion that Mayor Bowron and Cooper had knowledge Friday of the location of the dictograph in Mr. Cunningham's private office. If Cooper has affidavits disclosing the identity of the guilty parties, it is his duty as a law enforcing officer and as a private citizen to make their names known and to publish the affidavits in order that the guilty persons, whoever they might be, can be prosecuted.[11]

Bowron backed off from his accusations and, a few days later, won reelection by a wide margin.

George Francis stayed in private practice until his death in 1950, which was surrounded by bizarre circumstances. On March 16, 1950, campers came upon his new sedan in the Deep Creek campground on the north slopes of the San Bernardino Mountains in Inyo County. In the backseat they observed Francis lying dead with his head placed on a pillow, as though he had simply fallen asleep. Apparently he had gone to visit his brother James in Inyo, having just returned from a trip to Mexico. On that trip, the boat from which he and his friends were fishing had been beached in a storm and they had to spend the night in a damp cave. Because of this ordeal, argued his friends and family, Francis developed pneumonia, and therefore his death in his car should be ruled an accident. Over the next few years, his family and law partners battled Lloyds of London insurers in the courts, charging that Francis's death was an accident.

The reason for this protracted battle became clear in a California Supreme Court decision in 1954. The details are murky, but in late 1949 Francis's firm sent him down to South America to deliver $175,000 of negotiable securities. The firm took out two accident-travel policies on his life, in case of a plane crash or other disaster. Francis returned in early March 1950 and then went to visit his brother to "take some sun." Two days later he was dead. His colleagues argued that they should be able to collect on the policies because his death was an accident caused by the motorboat failure and the subsequent exposure.

The Supreme Court ruled in favor of Lloyds of London. Before Francis was cremated, the insurer's lawyers argued, the coroner found medication and alcohol in his system. Moreover, the plaintiffs declined to report the death to the insurer in a timely fashion so that they could perform their own investigation. Had he been a ghostly observer, Francis may have been dismayed to see that because of this court case, California case law now held that plaintiffs had the burden of proving that death was an accident, instead of insurance companies having to prove that it wasn't.[12]

Deputy District Attorney George Stahlman resigned in 1939 in what the *Long Beach Independent* called a "forerunner of political scandals that will rock Los Angeles." In his resignation letter, Stahlman accused Buron Fitts of trying to muzzle investigation into alleged county political graft by removing him from the case. Bowron came to Stahlman's defense: "I know nothing at all relative to the facts in this case . . . but I do know George Stahlman. . . . I know his integrity and his courage, and I class him as one of the best deputies who has served in the office of the district attorney in recent years."[13] Stahlman opened a private practice with Grant Cooper, representing celebrities such as Walter Pidgeon and Robert Mitchum and such underworld figures as Mickey Cohen and madam Ann Forrester. One of Stahlman's first high-profile clients was Clifford Clifton, who fended off suits from Fitts, who—in turn—hoped to intimidate the "Cafeteria King."

In 1953 Stahlman moved to San Diego County, where he still practiced law occasionally but mostly spent time tending to his twenty-seven-acre avocado ranch and raising peacocks. "The Hangman" passed away in 1978.

Tom White's beleaguered sister, Violet, divorced her first husband after the trial. She remarried and moved to Bountiful, Utah, where she lived quietly and, according to her stepchildren, never spoke of her brother or Burmah White. She died in 1980.

Joseph Adams died on January 7, 1935, of appendicitis at age fifty-six. Pearl was left to raise Jo Louraine on her own and, by all accounts, did an exemplary job, especially without the benefit of income from husband or grown daughter. The stress of Burmah's arrest, trial, and incarceration, in addition to her husband's frailty and then death, was almost too much for her to bear. She often wrote to Burmah's parole board, at times pleading for mercy for her daughter but more often arguing that Burmah was also a victim:

> *It fell on her young shoulders to prove that it was through fear for her life and the lives of others in her family that kept her from saying anything. . . . She was little more than a child in the hands of a hard, merciless, criminal and she learned his true character and was drawn into his crimes almost at the same time and I realize it would require a good supply of real nerve to defy the desires of such a man, we only have to remember the fiendish, brutal shooting of Miss Withington to realize that he would stop at nothing.*

Furthermore, Pearl argued, it would have been impossible for her daughter to get a fair trial in Los Angeles County at that time—most certainly referring to the public outrage for the crimes of the Whites. No matter where the trial was held or the outcome, she added, Bowron's sentence was way too harsh—harsher than any reasonable person would have implemented. Still, it may not have gone over very well with the parole board when she sent the following to it before one of her hearings in the mid-1930s:

> *Of all the victims of Tom White, Burmah is the big loser. Some lost a little money, some lost other valuables and one poor lady lost her eyesight (and my heart goes out to her), but Burmah lost everything: reputation, good name and all, condemned and glaringly held up to the world by some of the filthy newspapers as a "bandit's moll" and finally hustled through an unfair trial and given a sentence that would have been plenty severe for Tom White himself. Then add to this the brutal treatment she suffered at his hands; there were times when her body was practically covered with bruises. It hardly seems like fair play to say the least.*[14]

148

Jo Louraine Adams was popular at school, active on her junior high and high school student councils and in dramatic arts. Eerily mirroring her older sister's childhood experience, on March 2, 1942, when she was eighteen years old, Jo Louraine was a passenger in a friend's car when a drunk driver hit it. The extent of her injuries is not known, but she did spend a few days in the hospital, after which she recovered. She married a few months later, though that marriage and a subsequent one both ended after less than two years. In 1955 she married once again and moved with her husband to Minnesota, where she helped raise a stepson and lived a quiet life as a homemaker until her death in 1994.

Charles "Crombie" Allen recovered from the neck wounds inflicted upon him by Tom White. He continued his work with Rotary Club International and established journalism and oratorical scholarships for teens and young adults in Ontario, California, high schools and junior colleges. He did fund-raising for Casa Colina, a convalescent home for disabled children, and during World War II started a marketing campaign to encourage juveniles to purchase war savings stamps. He was a member of Sigma Delta Chi, a national professional journalism fraternity, and was posthumously elected to the California Newspaper Hall of Fame in 1985. A year or two after Cora Withington fully recovered from her wounds, minus her sight, Allen proposed marriage to her. Withington turned him down, not wishing to be a burden to anyone.

Cora Belle Withington made an impression on people long before she became famous as a victim of Tom and Burmah White. A brilliant woman, Withington completed three years of college at the Greensburg Lutheran Seminary near Pittsburgh, Pennsylvania, before money ran dry and she decided to move to Southern California, where there was more opportunity for a young, single woman. She had already been teaching in Los Angeles for twenty years before Tom White's bullet struck her in the head. Withington, though she never again would be able to see, spent the rest of her life trying to help others do so. She worked with Los Angeles and Indiana, Pennsylvania, businessmen to procure eyeglasses for those who could not afford them. Withington passed away in 1969 at age eighty-seven.[15]

A week after Burmah's trial ended, Detective William "Chester" Burris received a letter from Cora Withington, written for her by her sister, thanking him for his donation to her fund. She regretted she could not meet him in person because she was still too fragile from her wounds: "The giving of the reward given you for risking your life in the performance of your duty has made a warm glow in my heart which will always remain. I hope, my dear Mr. Burris, that your kindness to me will return to you some day in some way, a hundred-fold."[16]

Perhaps kindness returned to Burris privately, but publicly he earned accolades for his success as a detective. Burris was recognizable (at least in name) by citizenry for his part in the Whites' capture, but the following year he would become even more famous in the public eye for his role in apprehending kidnappers of millionaire William Gettle of Arcadia. The kidnappers demanded a sixty-thousand-dollar ransom for the return of Gettle, which Mrs. Gettle agreed to pay. However, before the money was paid, Burris and a fellow detective broke the case after installing a Dictaphone in the home of a bank robbery suspect. Information from the Dictaphone led them to a La Crescenta home where Gettle was being held. He was returned, unharmed, to his family on the eve of May 14, 1934. Burris retired in the mid-1950s and passed away in Humboldt, California, in 1962.[17]

By the time Ellery Cuff retired from the Los Angeles public defender's office in 1963 to care for his ailing son, he had defended more than four thousand accused criminals. From a statistical standpoint, every public defender who works in a major city long enough will probably wind up shielding a high-profile client. Cuff, however, wound up with at least half a dozen: Louise Peete, a mass murderer executed in 1947 whom he always respectfully referred to as "Mrs. Peete"; Albert W. Dyer, who killed three young girls in 1937; and William O. Dullin, who in 1936 Cuff proved had been wrongfully convicted of murdering prizefighter Mickey Erno.

Cuff never publicly spoke of Burmah's pardon case and of course never spoke about clients to family and friends. But his grand-niece maintained that each and every case was important to him, and he treated them all as if they were his only one. In many ways, Cuff was ahead of his time: He was especially concerned about convicted women, people of color, and poor people, who did not always have adequate representation in court. In his experience, Cuff said, looking back at his career at a 1963 conference, thorough recordkeeping by the government has certainly helped law enforcement, but not necessarily prisoners seeking rehabilitation when they finished their time served. "We hold his past over him like a sword, ready to cut him down anytime he tries to get a decent job. . . . I notice that most European countries declare an amnesty after a man has been out of prison so many years and kept his nose clean."[18]

Of course, Burmah Adams White Dymond did not necessarily fit Cuff's mold for the downtrodden convicted. She was able to obtain a good job for a time after prison and was able to remarry and live in relative obscurity for the rest of her life. Certainly Burmah was an alcoholic. As of this writing, many California and Washington State prison and parole records are not available for scrutiny by the general public, so it is not possible to know whether or how her struggles with alcohol might have led to her lack of employment and fulfillment in Washington or whether it was just her record as a convict that kept her from finding these things. Or neither. For that matter, we cannot know whether substance abuse played a part in her crimes with Tom White, though it seems likely.

The people involved in Burmah Adams White's arrest and trial cut a cross section of Los Angeles politics, jurisprudence, and law enforcement that would go down in history as one of the most corrupt in metropolitan history. For the most part, the scores of people involved with Burmah's arrest and trial were not concerned with justice so much as they were with creating a new bureaucracy to deal with the real and imagined chaos of a city growing exponentially even during the Great Depression.

At the same time, the activities of the "Blonde Rattlesnake" satiated the need of America's newspapers and radio, which desperately needed sensational content to feed a public that wanted to know "when" and "how," but mostly "why"—and to be entertained while trying to come to some conclusion about that. In turn, this public—consumers of mass media like radio shows and columnist-driven accounts in the newspaper and magazines—could try to work out their anxieties about a society that was seemingly increasingly violent and encroaching upon their front yards.

And the anxiety was real. Her feature in *Calling All Cars* and other radio programs and myriad newspaper columns were certainly entertaining, but Burmah's story also forced residents of Los Angeles and other cities to ask themselves, "If this girl from a 'regular family' could so easily fall in with a criminal like Tom White, who's to say my child couldn't also?"

Today, society still asks one basic question when men and women are convicted of violence or fraud perpetrated over days, weeks, months or years—anything that isn't considered a spontaneous act. That question is about his or her romantic partner, and it is always some form of "Why did she/he go along with it and not say anything . . . or just walk away?" There are as many answers as there are human beings, but usually they fall into some general categories: abuse, fear of abuse, physical injury, addiction, religious fervor, or some kind of abnormal psychology.

Also true today is that society still tries to gauge these answers by looking at the lover's image on television or in photographs. It is human nature to try to form an opinion about someone's actions by assessing an image created in a nanosecond of someone's life, and to arrive at a conclusion about that person's motivations without having any information about the rest of his or her entire life.

The "Blonde Rattlesnake" may have been baffled too.

ENDNOTES

Author's Note

1 *The St. Louis Star and Times*, January 31, 1938, 9.
2 *Los Angeles Times*, November 12, 1933, 16.
3 Ibid.

Introduction

1 "Dragnet Used in Allen Case," *Los Angeles Times*, August 18, 1933, A1; "Bandits Death Told at Trial," *Los Angeles Times*, October 28, 1933, A8.
2 "Officers Raid Four Clubs . . . ," *Los Angeles Times*, September 1, 1933, A1.
3 "Gigantic Drive Launched to Halt Gang Activities," *Los Angeles Times*, September 8, 1933, A1.
4 Nettie J. Yaw, "What We Can Do to Stop Crime!," *Los Angeles Times*, March 25, 1934, H11.
5 See "Enigma Woman: Nellie Madison, Femme Fatales and Noir Fiction," *Montana, the Magazine of Western History* (Spring 2004).
6 Ibid.
7 Ibid.
8 "Criminal Registry Law Passed by Supervisors . . . ," *Los Angeles Times*, September 12, 1933, A1; "Felon Listing Starts Today . . . ," *Los Angeles Times*, September 13, 1933, A1.
9 "Secret Parole System Scored," *Los Angeles Times*, November 8, 1933, A8.
10 Ibid.
11 *The People of the State of California v. Burmah A. White*, California State Archives, Office of the Secretary of State, Sacramento.
12 Los Angeles Public Library Images, *Herald Examiner* Collection, HE box 4818.

Chapter 1   But Is It Love?

1 Her parole records show that she scored 123 on the Stanford-Binet IQ test, though it is not clear at what age she took the exam.
2 *Santa Ana Register*, February 27, 1926–September 1, 1929.
3 Jerry Bowen, "Great Depression Caused Hard Times in Solano," April 5, 2008: http://www.solanoarticles.com/history/index.php/weblog/more/great_depression_caused_hard_times_in_solano/ (retrieved May 3, 2018).
4 Ibid.
5 *Santa Ana Register*, September 18 and 21, 1926; October 5, 1926.
6 *Santa Ana Register*, September 9, 1933.
7 Ibid.
8 White, Burmah A., No. 55120, California Department of Corrections Records, California State Archives, Office of the Secretary of State, Sacramento.
9 Military file of Thomas White, National Archives.
10 See Golden Pioneer Museum's *Pictures of America: Golden, Colorado* (Chicago: Arcadia Publishing, 2002) and Asylum Projects website: http://www.asylumprojects.org/index.php?title=Colorado_State_Industrial_School_for_Boys (retrieved May 3, 2018).

11 "Two Men Caught Robbing Register in Drug Store . . . ," *Colorado Springs Gazette*, September 1, 1916, 2; Corrections Records, Colorado Archives.
12 "Boy Flees Reformatory; Caught at Fort Logan," *Rocky Mountain News*, July 2, 1918, 10.
13 "Bandit Slain in Battle . . . ," *Los Angeles Times*, September 7, 1933; "Burglars Load Booty on Truck," July 16, 1930, A8; "Officers Land Cigarette Haul," *Los Angeles Times*, July 20, 1930, 15.
14 The detail about the glass eye seems to have been missed by contemporary newspapers, but magazines with longer lead times dug up this little fact. For example, "Calling All Cars: The Circle of Death," *Radio Guide*, June 2, 1934, 36–37. It was also discussed at trial.
15 "Inside the Heart of a Bandit Girl," *True Story* (May 1934), 50.
16 Ibid., 126.
17 Ibid.
18 *True Story*, 127.
19 Burmah A. White, No. 55120.

Chapter 2   Short Romance, Quick Death
1 "Couple Married Here to Make Home in San Francisco," *Santa Ana Register*, September 5, 1933, 10.
2 "Parents of White Girl Take Stand," *Santa Ana Register*, October 31, 1933, 1.
3 *People of the State of California v. Burmah A. White*, 332–3.
4 Ibid, 334–7.
5 Ibid, 454–54.
6 Parole file, Burmah A. White, No. 55120, 7.
7 In fact, White's police record as recounted by the *Los Angeles Daily News* showed that on April 24, 1933, Dillon reported to the state parole office that her brother had left the state and she did not know his whereabouts. Any punishment for White for this violation of his parole is not recorded. "Here Is Record of Gunman Who Scorned Alias," *Los Angeles Daily News*, Burris Family Scrapbook (not dated, but most likely September 8 or 9, 1933).
8 Ibid.
9 *People of the State of California v. Burmah A. White*, 480–3.
10 Burmah and Tom White lived too far east in Los Angeles to be considered within the West Los Angeles division boundaries. However, most of their crimes were committed in West Los Angeles, so the case fell under McCaleb's purview.
11 *People of the State of California v. Burmah A. White*, 466.
12 According to Kathleen Cairns, favored high-profile inmates at Tehachapi were allowed to sell their stories to pulp detective magazines for fifty dollars, and presumably this is what Burmah was paid by *True Story*. Cairns refers to those convicted of murder, but Burmah's notoriety (and her looks) earned her many publishing offers as well. The first-person stories were actually penned by ghostwriters. In Burmah's case, it is obvious the interviewer spent a great deal of time with her. Many of the assertions in the article can be backed up with reliable evidence.

13 *True Story*, 129.
14 Ibid., 128.
15 Ibid., 131–2.
16 Ibid., 132.
17 Ibid.
18 From LAPD/Burmah White robbery report taken by William Chester Burris, courtesy Burris Family scrapbooks.
19 "Bandit Slain in Battle; Blonde Bride Captured," *Los Angeles Times*, September 7, 1933, part II, 1; "Blonde Widow Defies Police," September 8, 1933, part II, 1.
20 Los Angeles Public Library Photo Archives.
21 *True Story*, 132.
22 "Six Officers Praised for Part in Capture," *Los Angeles Times*, September 13, 1933, 28.

Chapter 3   Pretrial

1 Letter from Burmah White to lawyers, November 4, 1933, *Herald-Examiner* Collection, Los Angeles Public Library.
2 "Bandit Slain in Battle: Blonde Bride Captured," *Los Angeles Times*, September 7, 1933, A1.
3 "Blonde Widow Defies Police," *Los Angeles Times*, September 8, A1.
4 Ibid.
5 Letter from Emily D. Latham, secretary of the State Board of Prison Trustees, n.d., possibly to trustee Lotus Loudon, in whose records the letter is found. Rose Viola Pickerel was the first woman LAPD officer to work a beat with a male patrolman and organized the first Board of Education program for women prisoners.
6 *State of California v. Burmah White*, 476–8.
7 California State Archives, Prison Records, Burmah White, No. 55120.
8 "Changes Mind about Talking," *Santa Ana Register*, September 8, 1933, 1.
9 *Los Angeles Times*, May 2–December 8, 1929.
10 Los Angeles Public Library, Photo Collection, *Herald-Examiner* Collection, HE box 4818, 1933. The *Los Angeles Herald and Express* and the *Evening Herald* merged in 1931 to create the *Los Angeles Herald and Express*. Later, in 1962, the *Los Angeles Examiner* merged with the *Los Angeles Herald and Express* and became the *Los Angeles Herald Examiner*. It went defunct in 1989.
11 Los Angeles Public Library, Photo Collection, *Herald-Examiner* Collection, HE box 4818, 1933.
12 Letter from Buron Fitts to James Davis, September 14, 1933, Burris Family Collection.
13 Policewoman Rose Pickerel later told parole officer Emily Latham that Burmah "showed no sorrow over her husband's death, did not cry" when she was first taken into custody, and that it was Pickerel's opinion that "she did not care for him." Of course outward displays of grief and trauma were not widely understood at this time and within the context of court and parole records.
14 For more on Fitts, see Jules Tygiel, *The Great Los Angeles Swindle: Oil, Stocks and Scandal During the Roaring Twenties* (Berkeley: University of California Press, 1996).

15 See Cecilia Rasmussen, "D.A. Fitts Was Good Match for the Scandalous '30s," *Los Angeles Times*, September 19, 1999, 3; Ted Thackrey, "Former Dist. Atty. Buron Fitts Found Shot to Death at Home," *Los Angeles Times*, March 30, 1973, D7.

16 Ibid.

17 See Rasmussen, "D.A. Fitts Was Good Match for the Scandalous '30s," *Los Angeles Times*, September 19, 1999, 3; Thackrey, "Former Dist. Atty. Buron Fitts Found Shot to Death at Home," *Los Angeles Times*, March 30, 1973, D7.

18 See Rasmussen, "D.A. Fitts Was Good Match for the Scandalous '30s," *Los Angeles Times*, September 19, 1999, 3.

19 Ibid.

20 Ibid.

21 Tygiel, *The Great Los Angeles Swindle: Oil, Stocks and Scandal During the Roaring Twenties*, 261–2.

22 "Grand Jury Will Hear Bandit Case," *Los Angeles Times*, September 11, 1933, A1.

23 "Blonde Bandit True Bill Near," *Los Angeles Times*, September 13, 1933, A1.

24 Ibid.

25 "Blonde Bandit True Bill Near," *Los Angeles Times*, September 13, 1933, A12.

26 E-mail correspondence with Diane Dixon, granddaughter of Egbert Earl Moody, January 15, 2018. In possession of the author.

27 Los Angeles Public Library, *Herald-Examiner* Collection, HE Box 4818, 1933.

Chapter 4   Pop Culture

1 George Lait, "Calling All Cars: The Circle of Death," *Radio Guide*, June 2, 1934.

2 One can hear the Burmah White episode of this radio program here: https://www.youtube.com/watch?v=pkIYjIRKMlc (accessed May 4, 2018).

3 "Law Forces Join Hands to Drive Out Gangsters," *Los Angeles Times*, September 1, 1933, A1; Albert Nathan, "Chief Davis to Carry War to the Criminal . . . ," *Los Angeles Times*, August 27, 1933, 6.

4 "On Their Way: Thousand Thieves Headed for This City," *Los Angeles Times*, December 1, 1913, 9.

5 "Law Forces Join Hands to Drive Out Gangsters," *Los Angeles Times*, September 1, 1933, 1.

6 See, for example, Mary June Burton, "The Runaway Boy Who Became Our Chief of Police," *Los Angeles Times Sunday Magazine*, September 24, 1933, 3.

7 Joe Domanick, *To Protect and to Serve: The LAPD's Century of War in the City of Dreams* (New York: Pocket Books, 1994), 52.

8 For more on Davis and Los Angeles's early years, see Kenneth Starr, *Material Dreams: Southern California through the 1920s* (Oxford, England: Oxford University Press, 1991).

9 Website, Los Angeles Police Foundation: http://www.lapdonline.org/history_of_the_lapd/content_basic_view/1109. See also *The Encyclopedia of Police Science*, ed. William G. Bailey (New York: Taylor & Francis, 1995), 411–15.

10 Albert Nathan, "Chief Davis to Carry War to the Criminal . . . ," *Los Angeles Times*, August 27, 1933, 6.

11 For a comprehensive study on radio programs and Depression-era police departments, see Kathleen Battles, *Calling All Cars: Radio Dragnets and the Technology of Policing* (Minneapolis: University of Minnesota Press, 2010).

12 "Dial Opens Local Police Drama," *Los Angeles Times*, November 29, 1933, 16.

13 George Lait, "Calling All Cars: The Circle of Death," *Radio Guide*, June 2, 1934.

14 "Artificial Emotion," *Los Angeles Times*, November 7, 1933, A4.

15 Actor Ricardo Cortez's most famous role at this time was as Sam Spade in *The Maltese Falcon* (1931). There is no evidence to support the notion that Tom White tried to shoot Cortez. This rumor may have stemmed from the fact that a casting agent named Tom White worked on a Cortez film some years prior.

16 Syndicated. For example, it ran in the *Syracuse* (New York) *Journal*, September 24, 1933, 8.

17 For an in-depth study of Nellie May Madison's ordeal and Aggie Underwood's interviews with her and other female criminals in Los Angeles, see Joan Renner (au.) and Christina Rice (ed.), *The First with the Latest! Aggie Underwood, the Los Angeles Herald, and the Sordid Crimes of a City* (Los Angeles: Photo Friends of the Los Angeles Public Library, 2015).

18 This is not clear, because she was obviously eligible for parole, though she was denied. Unfortunately, her medical records were destroyed, so it is not possible to know what she suffered from.

19 Agness Underwood, "Burmah White Pays for Wrongs in Bitterness," *Los Angeles Evening Herald and Express*, April 3, 1935, 1.

20 Burmah White, as told to James Shambra, "Terror Bandit's Blonde 'Moll' Tells Her Own Life Story," *Los Angeles Evening Herald and Express*, September 12, 1933, 1.

21 City directories from 1931 to 1933 suggest this was true.

22 Ibid.

23 Michele Hilmes, *Only Connect: A Cultural History of Broadcasting in the United States* (Boston: Wadsworth/Cengage Learning, 2013), 101.

24 Dansville (New York) *Breeze*, April 12, 1934.

25 *Radio Mirror*, 72

26 *Santa Ana Register*, November 6, 1933, 10; Los Angeles Public Library, *Los Angeles Evening Herald and Express* photographs, *Herald-Examiner* Collection, HE Box 4818, photo record no. 3, second caption.

27 Burmah White episode of *Calling All Cars*: https://www.youtube.com/watch?v=pkIYjIRKMlc (accessed May 4, 2018).

Chapter 5   Trial, Part I

1 Lew Scarr column, *San Diego Union*, January 4, 1971, 8; Obituary, George Stahlman, Frank Rhoades column, *San Diego Union*, October 4, 1978, 28.

2 Due to public outcry, Madison's sentence was later reduced to life in prison; she was eventually released. See Kathleen Cairns, *The Enigma Woman: The Death Sentence of Nellie May Madison* (Lincoln, NE: Bison Books, 2009).

3 "Negro Is Said to Have $4,000,000 for Munitions," *San Francisco Chronicle*, February 16, 1918, 8; "Alice Rogers Out for Kale," *San Francisco Chronicle*, March 8, 1919, 7.

4 The building was demolished and rebuilt in 1936, owing to the significant damage inflicted upon it by the 1933 Long Beach earthquake.

5 *People of the State of California v. Burmah A. White*, 1–21.

6 Los Angeles Public Library photo collection.

7 *People of the State of California v. Burmah A. White*, 12–13.

8 Ibid., 20–21.

9 "Charges Grow in Port Ouster," *Los Angeles Times*, January 27, 1933, 15; "Werner Ousts Port Suit Aide," *Los Angeles Times*, May 6, 1933, 15; "Mayor to Speed Harbor Actions," *Los Angeles Times*, May 7, 1933, 15; "City Files Suit in Harbor Sale," *Los Angeles Times*, May 13, 1933, 13. Francis was replaced by another aide, who helped file civil charges against certain companies. Notably, one of these companies was headed by importer Norton Simon, who at that time was building an empire by revitalizing under-valued businesses.

10 *People of the State of California v. Burmah White*, 21–27.

11 Burmah's attorney George Francis waived the defense's right to an opening statement. He did, however, reserve it for the defense when they made their case later.

12 See, for example: "Federal Rules of Evidence: Article VI—Witnesses," Cornell Law School website: https://www.law.cornell.edu/rules/fre/rule_615 (accessed April 30, 2018).

13 *People of the State of California v. Burmah White*, 186–92.

14 Ibid.

15 It is unclear who Chief Taylor and Inspector Slayton were, although he probably meant "Chief Davis."

16 *People of the State of California v. Burmah White*, 162–8.

17 Ibid., 179.

18 Ibid., 172.

19 Ibid., 181.

Chapter 6   Trial, Part II

1 *People of the State of California v. Burmah White*, 31–51.

2 Ibid., 68–76.

3 Ibid., 73–78.

4 Ibid., 78–92.

5 Ibid., 77–128.

6 Testimony of Dr. T. C. Low, *People of the State of California v. Burmah White*, 230–3.

7 *People of the State of California v. Burmah White*, 129–42.

8 "Alley Club Raided by Prohis, 1 Nabbed," *Nevada State Journal*, March 13, 1933, 8; "Prohi Violators Plead Guilty at Carson Hearings," *Nevada State Journal*, June 21, 1933, 6; "Car Stolen from Reno Man in L.A.; Woman Is Killed," *Nevada State Journal*, August 18, 1933, 4.

Chapter 7   Trial, Part III

1 *People of the State of California v. Burmah Adams White*, 313–24.

2 Ibid., 345–53.
3 Ibid., 360–9.
4 Ibid., 372–92.
5 Ibid.
6 Ibid., 407–16.
7 Ibid., 482–9.
8 Ibid., 458.
9 Ibid., 452–7.
10 Ibid., 471–4.

Chapter 8   Tehachapi

1 *State of California v. Burmah Adams White*, 513–5.
2 "Bandit Girl Smiles on Departure," *Los Angeles Examiner*, December 6, 1933, 1.
3 "Burmah White Likes Prison at Tehachapi," *Bakersfield Californian*, December 8, 1933, 13.
4 Cairns, *Hard Time at Tehachapi: California's First Women's Prison* (Albuquerque: University of New Mexico Press, 2009), 23.
5 Ibid. Cairns uses this quote from the *Los Angeles Times*, January 1911.
6 Ibid.
7 Harry Carr, "The Lancer" column, *Los Angeles Times*, March 12, 1934, A1.
8 Ibid.
9 Barbara Miller, "Honor System Rules Women at Tehachapi," *Los Angeles Times*, July 12, 1937, A1.
10 Carr, "The Lancer" column, *Los Angeles Times*, March 12, 1934, A1.
11 Ibid.
12 Gilbert Brown, *Los Angeles Post-Record*, July 15, 1935, n.p. From clipping file attached to Burmah White's parole record: White, Burmah A., No. 55120, California Secretary of State Archives.
13 Ibid.
14 Agness Sullivan Underwood, *Newspaperwoman* (New York: Harper, 1949), 157.
15 Agness Underwood, "Burma White Pays Debt for Wrongs in Bitterness," *Los Angeles Herald and Express*, April 3, 1935, 2. This series of articles sometimes varied in versions because it was syndicated by International News Service. For example, this last line that ends with "eighteen years" does not appear in the *Herald and Express* but rather in a version edited for the *San Francisco Call-Bulletin*.
16 Cairns, *Hard Time at Tehachapi*, 61.
17 Underwood, "Life of 'Forgotten' Women in Tehachapi Prison Told," *Los Angeles Herald and Express*, March 29, 1935, 3.
18 Ibid.
19 Ibid.; Cairns, *Hard Time at Tehachapi*, 66.
20 Underwood, "Life of 'Forgotten' Women in Tehachapi Prison Told," *Los Angeles Herald and Express*, March 29, 1935, 3.
21 The appeals decision was handed down March 20, 1934; Underwood's interview was within days of this, given that the story ran April 3.

22 Underwood, "Burmah White Pays Debt for Wrongs in Bitterness," *Los Angeles Evening Herald and Express*, April 3, 1935, 2.

23 Ibid., 3.

24 White, Burmah A., No. 55120, 8.

25 Ibid., 3.

26 Ibid., 5.

27 Ibid., 3.

28 Burmah White was denied parole five times.

29 Barbara Miller, "Honor System Rules Women at Tehachapi," *Los Angeles Times*, July 12, 1937, A1.

30 Cairns, "Writing for Their Lives: The Clarion and Inmates at the California Institution for Women, Tehachapi," *Western Legal History*, vol. 21, no. 3 (Winter/Spring: 2008), 9.

31 Cairns, repeating quote by Warden Monahan in support of inmates' work on the paper, "Writing for Their Lives: The *Clarion* and Inmates at the California Institution for Women, Tehachapi," *Western Legal History*, vol. 21, no. 3 (Winter/Spring: 2008), 10.

32 See, for example, "State Board Denies Burmah White Parole," *San Bernardino County Sun*, August 21, 1936, 12.

33 "Burmah White, Gangster's Bride from Santa Ana Is Now Poetess in Prison," *Santa Ana Register*, July 10, 1935, 1.

34 It is not clear whether Warden Monahan was attempting to cast a positive or negative light on Burmah's character and rehabilitation when she made the following comment in one of Burmah's parole reports—though it is very clear what she thought of Burmah's fellow inmate: "The most surprising thing about this woman is that she selects Florence Inman, a low grade person, as her most intimate friend and constant companion." White, Burmah A., No. 55120, California State Archives, 9.

35 White, Burmah A., No. 55120.

36 Ibid.

37 Ibid., 8–10.

38 Ibid., 11.

Chapter 9   The Malignancy of This Thing

1 "Bare Secret Parole of Burmah White," *Los Angeles Evening Herald and Express*, February 7, 1942, n.p.

2 Cairns, *Hard Time at Tehachapi*, 118.

3 Edmond Herrscher papers (Collection 1829), UCLA Library Special Collections, Charles E. Young Research Library, UCLA. Herrscher frequently appeared in headlines throughout the 1940s and 1950s for his marital and romantic life and his business dealings. In one instance, in 1951, a young model sued him for paternity, though he maintained that he was sterile.

4 "Locksmith Called to Help Serve Papers in Suit," *Oakland Tribune*, April 8, 1943, 31; "Mate Emptied Mansion," *Oakland Tribune*, January 31, 1947, 17.

5 "Speeding Auto Crashes Bus," *Oakland Tribune*, October 26, 1949, 20.

6 The author thanks Cuff's grand-niece, Vivian Girot, for this information. (Phone interview with Vivian Girot, January 28, 2018. Notes in possession of the author.)

7 The City of Los Angeles established the job of police court defender, which then became the Los Angeles City public defender's office.

8 David Sokol, "First for the Defense," *Los Angeles Times* Sunday Magazine, December 3, 1933, 11.

9 "Defender for Sirhan Regarded as the Best," *Los Angeles Times*, June 17, 1968, 19.

10 Charles Samuels, "Startling Story of Love, Crime, Flight, and Woman's Undying Devotion," *Fresno Bee*, November 12, 1933, 20; "Drink Fails as Excuse for Slayer," *Los Angeles Times*, May 19, 1934, 14.

11 "Applicant's Statement," Department of Corrections and Rehabilitation records, Pardon Application File, Burmah A. White, No. 55120, California State Archives, Office of the Secretary of State, Sacramento, California.

12 "Divorces Asked," *Seattle Daily Times*, December 22, 1953, 34.

13 Classified Section, *Los Angeles Daily Journal*, October 20–November 30, 1955; Burmah A. White, No. 55120, California State Archives.

14 Burmah A. White, No. 55120, California State Archives.

15 Employment record, Department of Corrections and Rehabilitation records, Pardon Application File, Burmah A. White, No. 55120, California State Archives, Office of the Secretary of State, Sacramento, California.

16 Letter from E. W. Lester to Goodwin J. Knight, November 5, 1956, Department of Corrections and Rehabilitation Records, Pardon Application File, Burmah A. White, No. 55120, California State Archives, Office of the Secretary of State, Sacramento, California.

17 Extract of letter from Thad F. Brown to Governor Knight, Department of Corrections and Rehabilitation Records, Pardon Application File, Burmah A. White, No. 55120, California State Archives, Office of the Secretary of State, Sacramento, California.

18 Letter from Judge David Coleman to E. A. Burkhart, Adult Authority, August 5, 1955, Department of Corrections and Rehabilitation Records, Pardon Application File, White, Burmah A., No. 55120, California State Archives, Office of the Secretary of State, Sacramento, California.

19 Letter from Thomas C. Yager to Burmah A. Dymond, December 18, 1957. Department of Corrections and Rehabilitation records, Pardon Application File, Burmah A. White, No. 55120, California State Archives, Office of the Secretary of State, Sacramento, California.

20 Her intake papers for San Quentin (she was there for a short time until transferred to Tehachapi) note "liquors" where it asks about "habits." It isn't clear if this is merely recreational drinking, or something more serious. Department of Corrections and Rehabilitation Records, Pardon Application File, Burmah A. White, No. 55120, California State Archives, Office of the Secretary of State, Sacramento, California.

21 Death certificate, Burmah ARLINE Dymond, September 10, 1962, State of Washington Department of Health.

22 "Deaths," *Seattle Times*, December 12, 1962, 72.

Chapter 10   Vanished from Public View

1 "Officers Get Five Suspects on Clew Found . . . ," *Los Angeles Times*, November 1, 1933, 20.

2 Letter, Mrs. Edwin M. Porter to Detective W. C. Burris, September 8, 1933. Burris Family scrapbook.

3 "Secret Parole System Is Widely Condemned," *Los Angeles Herald and Express*, November 4, 1933, page unknown, Burris Family scrapbook.

4 "Bowron on Parole," *Los Angeles Times*, November 12, 1933, 16.

5 "Parole Ills Pointed Out," *Los Angeles Times*, June 27, 1935, 1.

6 For more on Bowron, see Tom Sitton, *Los Angeles Reformed: Fletcher Bowron's Urban Reform Revival, 1938–1953* (Albuquerque: University of New Mexico Press), 2005.

7 Joe Domanick, "Public Corruption, L.A.-Style . . . ," *Los Angeles Times*, January 25, 1998, "The State" section: M6.

8 Ibid.

9 *Los Angeles Times*, January 9–30, 1943, February 1–4, 1943, June 19, 1943, 15.

10 "Deputy DA Loses Life in 200-Foot Cliff Plunge," *Los Angeles Times*, June 19, 1955, 1.

11 "Three Linked to Spy Plot," *Los Angeles Times*, May 5, 1941, 2.

12 "Attorney's Death Not Accidental," *Los Angeles Times*, October 11, 1951, 25; "Claimants Must Prove Cause of Death," *Los Angeles Times*, March 20, 1954, 2.

13 "Resignation Touches off Sensation in District Attorney's Office, *Long Beach Independent*, August 14, 1939, 16.

14 White, Burmah A., No. 55120.

15 Background courtesy of Diane Dixon, granddaughter of Withington's friends, Mr. and Mrs. E. Earl Moody, e-mails dated January 11–15, 2018, in possession of the author; the *Indiana Progress*, July 12, 1899, 1; the *Indiana Gazette*, November 22, 1941, 3; Ancestry.com. *U.S., Social Security Death Index*, 1935–2014, Provo, UT: Ancestry.com Operations Inc., 2014.

16 Letter from Cora Belle Withington to William Chester Burris, November 14, 1933, Burris family scrapbook.

17 "Gettle Rescued Unharmed; Raiders Trap Five Suspects," *Los Angeles Times*, May 15, 1934, 1.

18 "Creed of Defender: Individual Sanctity," *Los Angeles Times*, April 28, 1963, sec. F, "Crime and Punishment," 4.

INDEX

ABOUT THE AUTHOR

Julia Bricklin has authored a dozen articles in well-respected commercial and academic journals, such as *Civil War Times*, *Financial History*, *Wild West*, *True West*, and *California History*, and spent several years contributing to Forbes.com. Bricklin grew up in Southern California, obtained a journalism degree at Cal Poly, San Luis Obispo, and worked in the TV/film industry for fifteen years before obtaining her master's degree in history at Cal State Northridge. In addition to serving as associate editor of *California History*, the publication of the California Historical Society, she is a professor of history at Glendale Community College. She lives in Studio City, California.